Cockatiels

Cockatiels as pets

Cockatiel book for Keeping, Pros and Cons, Care, Housing, Diet and Health.
by

Donald Sunderland

ALL RIGHTS RESERVED. This book contains material protected under International and Federal Copyright Laws and Treaties.

Any unauthorized reprint or use of this material is strictly prohibited. No part of this book may be reproduced or transmitted in any form or by any means, electronic, mechanical or otherwise, including photocopying or recording, or by any information storage and retrieval system without express written permission from the author.

Copyright © 2018

Published by: Zoodoo Publishing

Table of Contents

Table of Contents 3

Chapter 1: About Cockatiels 6

Chapter 2: Sourcing a Cockatiel 20

Chapter 3: Preparing your home for a cockatiel 34

Chapter 4: The cockatiel and his new home 49

Chapter 5: Cockatiel Care and Bonding 58

Chapter 6: Breeding your cockatiel 75

Chapter 7: Proper Cockatiel Healthcare 82

Chapter 8: Cost of Owning a Cockatiel 110

Conclusion 111

References 112

Introduction

Bringing a new bird home can be extremely exciting. However, one of the biggest mistakes that most bird enthusiasts make is to bring home a bird without considering the responsibilities that come with it. With birds like cockatiels, especially, the appearance and the adorable nature of the bird can be extremely tempting.

However, it is important to know a lot of things such as the right nutrition, care, health requirements and more to be a good bird parent. The personality of the breed that you pick should be feasible for you to handle with ease. You also need to be able to match your lifestyle with the requirements of the breed.

Cockatiels are known for their extremely social nature. They also make the best companion birds. Although they do not particularly love to be cuddled, these birds will need your time and attention. The temperament of these birds is responsible for their popularity as pets. They are a lot calmer than other birds of the same species. They also tend to be confident and curious birds. The adorable whistles and the ability to mimic certain words also make these birds extremely entertaining pets to have. They are able to learn and mimic calls of other birds and even the sound of vehicles, the ringing of a telephone or the alarm of a car.

They tend to be extremely goofy at times, as they play around and climb up and down their cage. Of course, these birds are beautiful to look at with the trademark Mohawk-like feather arrangement on their head.

There are several qualities of the cockatiel that make them wonderful pets, but there are some downsides as well. They can be demanding, can develop behavioral issues and even certain health issues when not maintained well by their owners.

This book gives you all the details of the personality and the quirks of this beautiful bird. It takes you step-by-step through the process of getting your bird comfortable in your home. All the details of proper nutrition and care required by these birds is mentioned in this book as well.

The idea is to ensure that you make a responsible decision when you think you are ready to open your home to a cockatiel. The book helps you decide if this bird is indeed the right one for your home.

Several cockatiels are abandoned each year because the families that bought or adopted them were not fully aware of the commitment it takes to raise a magnificent bird like this one. So, it is best that you gather as much information as you possibly can about these birds. This book is a complete guide for beginners and people who have some experience with other species of parrots.

You also have reference material that you can look up in order to expand your knowledge about the bird. Once you know for sure that you can make this commitment for 20-odd years, you can start your magical journey of raising a pet cockatiel.

Chapter 1: About Cockatiels

It is no secret that the cockatiel is the most popular choice among those who want to bring home a pet bird. These birds are funny, calm and extremely loving. They are full of personality, which makes them the ideal choice for someone who is looking for a companion bird.

This chapter tells you in detail about the physical traits of the bird, the personality and the history of this bird as a pet.

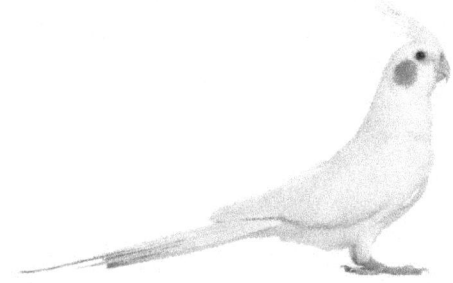

1. Physical characteristics

Cockatiels are also known as weiro or quarrions. These birds belong to the cockatoo family that is originally from Australia. These birds are quite easy to breed and are, hence, very popular as pets.

They are the only birds that are classified under the genus *Nymphicus*, under which they were considered to be a small cockatoo. However, they were classified as a subfamily, *Nymphicinae* after several molecular studies. Today, cockatiels are considered to be the smallest birds in the cockatoo family. They are native to the Australian bush lands, scrublands and wetlands.

The erect crest is the most distinctive physical trait of a cockatiel. It is also a sign of the bird's emotional state. The crest is almost vertical when the bird is excited or startled. It has an oblique or slanting shape when the bird is in a relaxed state. When the cockatiel is defensive or angry, the crest is held flat, close to the head. The crest is held flat even when the bird is exhibiting mating behavior. In this case, however, the ends of the crest protrude slightly at the back.

Unlike other cockatoos, the tail of the cockatiel is extremely long. The tail feathers are almost half the total length of the bird's body. On average, a cockatiel will grow up to a length of 30-33 cms. This makes it the smallest among all cockatoos, which may grow up to lengths of 60 cms.

The plumes of the wild or normal gray cockatiel are generally grey in color. The outer edges of the wings have a flash of white. The male has either a white face or a yellow face. The face of the female is normally light grey or completely gray in color.

Cheddar cheeks is one feature that is common to both the males and the females. This refers to a round area that is orange in color on the ears of the bird. In the case of a male cockatiel, this color is more pronounced. In the case of the females, it is often quite dull. These birds are sexually dimorphic, which means that you can tell the female apart from the male visually.

In general, cockatiels are very vocal birds. The male has a different call in comparison to the female. These birds can also be taught certain melodies. Cockatiels can be taught to repeat certain words. However, you cannot teach them to the same extent as some other species of parrots.

2. Mutations

For the first time ever, the normal gray or wild cockatiel was captively bred in France around the 1850's. These birds gained popularity across the globe almost instantly. For about 100 years, no mutations were observed in this species. The first mutation was the pied variety.

Mutation refers to a change in the genetic code of any living being. Today, you will find several color mutations in cockatiels. Any bird that differs from the normal grey one is the result of a mutation. Each color mutation holds a lot of significance in the popularity of that variety.

a) Two primary pigments

Coloration in cockatiels is the result of two specific pigments:

- **Melanin:** This is the pigment that gives the bird the distinct gray color. It is also seen in the beak, the feet and the eyes of the bird. This varies from one mutation to the other. For instance, in the case of the Lutino variety, melanin is absent. This makes the eyes of the bird red, as the blood vessels can be seen. The feet and the beak of the bird also appear lighter because of the lack of this commonly found pigment in cockatiels.

- **Lipochrome:** This pigment is responsible for the yellow coloration on the face of the bird. It also leads to the yellow coloration in the tail of the bird and the cheddar cheek formation on either ear of the bird. With maturity, the melanin pigment present in the face of the male bird becomes weaker. This allows the lipochrome to be seen more significantly. On the other hand, the melanin in the tail begins to increase, which makes the tail look solid and dark. In the case of the Whiteface mutation, the face appears white because lipochrome is absent. Any area that would otherwise be orange or yellow appears white in this mutation.

b) Types of mutations in cockatiels

There are three aspects that are affected by the genetic mutations in cockatiels. Based on this, there are three types of mutations:

- **Mutation of overall plumage color:** Besides the normal gray, there are other mutations that lead to changes in the color of the bird's plumage. These group colors are due to reduced levels of melanin in the bird's body:
  - Normal grey
  - Lutino
  - Cinnamon
  - Fallow
  - Recessive Silver
  - Dominant Silver
  - Emerald.

- **Coloration on the face:** One of the most distinct changes in the appearance of a cockatiel is the change in facial color. The color change is seen in the facial mask of the bird and/or the patch on the cheek. In the mutations listed below, there may also be a change in the overall color of the bird. In addition to that, the facial mask and the cheek coloration are also different:
  - Sex linked Yellow cheek
  - Dominant Yellow Cheek

- Whiteface
- Creamface
- Pastelface.

- **Changes in the pattern of the coloration:** The biggest and most significant change is seen on the back of the bird. This leads to a peculiar pattern in each type of mutation. There are alterations in other parts of the body and the plumage as well. However, the majority of the changes occur on the back. In the case of the pearl mutation, the pattern is usually uniform. It is possible that this pattern is incomplete in some cases. Pied mutations usually have random placements of feathers that are darker along with pied feathers. The clear, white and yellow feathers do not have any markings. In case there are no dark feathers on a pied variety, it is said to be clear of the presence of any pattern. The common patterned mutations are:
- Pied
- Pearl

c) Inheritance of various mutations:
There are three different ways in which a mutation is inherited by a cockatiel. These include:

- **Sex-linked inheritance:** These mutations occur in the X chromosome of the bird. Male cockatiels or cocks contain 2 X chromosomes. The hens or the female cockatiels contain one X and one Y chromosome. For the mutation to occur and become visibly evident, the X chromosome of both the parents should carry the mutation in the case of a cock. For the hen, the mutation should only be carried by one of the X chromosomes. It is not possible to see a split sex-linked mutation in females because the bird carries only one X chromosome. However, in the case of the male, split sex linked mutation is seen when only one of the two X chromosomes carries the sex-linked mutation. The sex linked mutations in cockatiels are:
- Pearl
-Cinnamon
-Yellow cheek
-Lutino.

- **Recessive mutation:** In order to have an offspring with a visual mutation, both the parents should have a gene that is either split or visual in mutation. Hens can also be split in the case of a split mutation. For instance, in order to produce a pied mutation, the parents should at least be split to a pied mutation. If one of the parents does not carry the gene for pied mutation, and the other one is of the visual pied variety, the offspring is split to pied. The common recessive mutations include:
  - Recessive silver
  - Whiteface
  - Pied
  - Fallow
  - Pastelface
  - Emerald.

- **Dominant mutations:** With dominant mutations it is enough for just one of the parents to carry the mutation in order to produce an offspring that is visual. The offspring can be male or female. In the case of a dominant mutation, the offspring cannot be split. There are only two options with this type of mutation - you either see it or you do not see it. You cannot have a dominant mutation that can be split into another mutation. The common dominant mutations seen in cockatiels include:
  - Normal Grey
  - Dominant Silver
  - Dominant Yellow Cheek
  - Dominant Pastelface.

These mutations have made the cockatiel even more popular as a pet bird. The various colorations that are seen have been appreciated by bird enthusiasts world over.

3. Distinguishing male from female

Distinguishing male cockatiels from females is relatively easy. To begin with, these birds have distinct physical traits that will help you tell the difference. There are also behavioral differences that you can rely on to tell a male cockatiel from a female.

Physical traits

Here are some of the most common differences between a male cockatiel and a female cockatiel:

The tail

- In adult females the tail feathers have markings on the underside.
- These markings appear in the form of dark or gray horizontal stripes or even white and gray stripes.
- Some females will also have irregular patterns or dots that are present on the gray plumes.
- If you do not see the markings instantly, you can also hold the tail against light and look closely.
- If markings are not seen, then it is a male bird.
- In the case of the Lutino mutation, the cheek circle is prominent even in the females. In this case, the presence of stripes and dots on the underside of tail and wing feathers is a clear indication of the gender of the bird. You will need bright light to examine the markings, however.

The face
- In the normal gray variety, the face has very striking features males.
- The orange spots on the cheeks stand out against the bright yellow facial feathers.
- The orange spots in females are usually lighter and may also be dull yellow in color or gray.
- In some varieties the yellow face in males only develops after molting. Until then, the face is brownish or gray in color.
- In the Whiteface mutation (the males that have non-white bodies) the males may not have the orange cheek spots at all while the females have a very faint cheek spot that is the same color as the rest of the body.

Body plumage
- In the normal grey variety, the plumes are darker in male birds and faint in females.
- This method of telling the difference is not as reliable, however. If you have any doubts after initial examination, this is a good way of telling the difference.

- You cannot identify the gender with this method in birds that have non-gray body plumes.
- In some mutations, you can also tell the difference by the faint yellow spots on the underside of the plumes on the females.
- In the case of the pearled cockatiels that have white dots on a body that is non-white, the dots on the male disappear after the first molt. These dots or pearls are retained in the females.

Veterinary examination
- This is the last and final test to determine the gender of the bird. This test should only be performed by a vet. Most often people injure their bird in an attempt to perform this test.
- The vet should be asked to sex the cockatiel.
- This includes an examination of the pelvic bones of the bird. The females tend to have a wider bone in order to lay eggs.
- This test is more reliable in the case of older birds. If you have rescued or bought a bird from a breeder, you may use this method. The older female would probably have laid eggs in the past, making the test easier and more accurate.
- A DNA test is the most reliable veterinary examination to determine the gender of the bird. The pelvic bone may differ from one individual to another, making this simple examination less accurate and less reliable if the bird is too young.

Behavioral traits
Like all species of birds and animals, male and female cockatiels also differ in their behavior quite a bit.

Vocalizations

- While it is not really true all the time, cockatiels that gain the ability to talk are most often males.
- Males are more vocal than females irrespective of their ability to talk, however.
- Male birds tend to whistle a lot more and vocalize while females are usually quiet.
- The vocalizations that are observed in females include screeching and hissing.

Reaction to a mirror
- Male cockatiels will respond more to a mirror. They will strut around, call out and even investigate the reflection more.
- Females will lose interest in the mirror very quickly.

Courtship rituals
- Male cockatiels exhibit more active courtship rituals. Sometimes, this behavior is seen even in the absence of a female.
- The bird will tap the beak on objects loudly in order to grab the attention of the female.
- They strut around tapping the beak and whistling. They will even hop or showcase head dips while doing so.
- The wing is lifted away from the body. This makes a heart shape when you look at it from behind.

Female courtship behavior
- In the case of females, courtship behavior is almost absent when a male is not present in the vicinity.
- They are not as active in creating a bond and courting.
- They tend to sit on a perch that is low, with the tail up. She appears to be peeping over the perch.
- She attempts to feed a male cockatiel that she has formed a bond with.

Masturbation methods
- Experienced owners will tell you that their birds often attempt to rub the vent area on their hand or on other objects.
- This is a habitual masturbation method that is seen in males mostly, but some females may also depict it. The methods are different.
- In the case of males, they will stand over the object and rub the vent area on it.
- Females tend to back up against the object, keeping the tail up and the body leaning forward.

Check on the egg laying
- Of course, it is the female that lays eggs. This examination is helpful when you have multiple birds in your cage.
- To be certain of the gender of the bird, you can place each one in a separate cage.

- You can even use a camera to record the behavior of the bird.
- Never provide a nesting box to a female who is less than 18 months old. Laying eggs very often leads to serious health issues in the younger birds.
- Do not remove the eggs, as it stimulates more egg laying.
- If the egg is fertilized, it means that you would have already observed the bonding activity in two birds. If you are not sure, this is a great method to check.

Knowing the gender of your bird will help you address several health and behavioral issues that may crop up in the future. It is especially important when you are planning to have multiple birds in your home.

4. Temperament and Behavior

Cockatiels are extremely hardy birds. They thrive well and can be bred quite easily as long as they have enough food. However, this is not the only reason why these birds are so popular. These birds have a temperament that is perfect for any beginner in the world of parrots.

They make excellent companion birds. The biggest advantage with cockatiels is that they can be hand-tamed quite easily. As a result, these birds are calmer around human beings. This is one of the main reasons why cockatiels are preferred pets for seniors. They are interactive, easy to manage and extremely friendly birds.

Cockatiels are vocal birds. The males, as discussed, tend to be more vocal than the females. These birds normally vocalize in the mornings and in the evenings. They chatter steadily and even make whistling sounds. However, these sounds are not disturbing to neighbors and the people at home. As a result, the cockatiel makes for the perfect apartment pet.

These birds are extremely intelligent. They are quiet easy to train as well. They love to be in the company of their owners, often accompanying them through the daily chores and activities. A pet cockatoo riding on the owner's shoulder is a very common sight. Sometimes, these birds perch on the head as well.

Cockatiels are also known for being extremely emotive. They will show you all their feelings such as fear, joy, sadness or anger by changing the position of the crest feathers. There is a lot to more to cockatiel behavior that we will learn about in the following sections. It is confusing at first. However, with careful observation, you will be able to understand why your bird exhibits certain behavior and what need you have to fulfill in order to satisfy your bird.

Cockatiels love to play. They are extremely active birds. They are also highly curious, which makes them even more delightful and entertaining as pets. They are able to keep themselves busy with activities like climbing as long as you provide them with all the right resources. They can be extremely goofy at times, hanging upside down from the cage bars or swinging on perches.

One common observation about the personality of the cockatiel is that they have all the best qualities of larger parrots like the cockatoo. However, they do not have the vices that these birds come with.

These birds form strong bonds with their owners. The males are more likely to cuddle than the females. Although, it is best to keep your interaction and petting limited to stroking the cheek or the torso of the bird. Unlike birds like cockatoos, these strong bonds with the owners do not lead to any possessive or jealous behavior on the part of the cockatiel. This makes them a lot safer to have in homes with children.

They are prone to some issues when they hit puberty. This includes screaming and nipping. However, these birds can be trained easily with some patience and the right techniques.

5. History of Cockatiels

Birds from the Cacatuinae sub-family are native to Australia. These birds also migrated to the Pacific and Asian regions. All through its history, Australia suffered from several seasons of dryness. During this time, several local species migrated to richer areas to look for food and water.

The cockatiel is also one of those species that spread in pursuit of food. Most of these species migrated in groups while one group stayed back in the native land. Because of the geographical separation and the isolation, these various groups were unable to reproduce together. This is possibly how cockatoos and cockatiels became separate species.

The Aboriginals used the cockatiels as a source of eggs and meat for a long time. However, the first ever report of the bird was made in the year 1770 by a British explorer and sailor named James Cook. This was when Australia was still known as "New Holland". His journals mention the presence of cockatiels in large numbers in the region. It also talks about one bird being taken to England along with his crew.

The earliest explorations of the interior regions of Australia can be traced back to the 1800s. This was when large numbers of the birds were exported to England. Several color mutations also appeared as the populations of this species began to spread far and wide.

During those times, there was very little knowledge about proper care of parrots and management of pet birds in general. As a result, the birds that were imported were subjected to a lot of stress and only a few of them survived because of improper care and management.

As a result, the Australian government proposed a ban on the import and export of flora and fauna. This ban is still applied, which means that wild animals from Australia cannot be exported to another country. As a result, the cockatiels that are found in the USA, Europe and Asia are bred in captivity. These birds have all descended from the ones that were imported back in the 1880s from the land Down Under.

How the bird got its name

In the year 1926, the name of the species was made official by the Royal Australasian Ornithologists Union. The name "cockatiel" was coined by a person named Jamrach. He derived the name from the Dutch word, "Kakatielje". This was a variant of the Portuguese word "cacatitho" used by the sailors back in the day. The name when translated means "little cockatoo"

History is filled with debates about the scientific name and the taxonomy of this bird. According to old literature, the cockatiel was also known as the "Cockatoo Parrot", "Crested Parakeet", "Corella" and "Yellow Top-knottes Parrot". On the other hand, the bird was known as "weero", "weiro" and "cockatiel" in Australia. There is also an Eastern version of the name which is "quarrion". The bird is also known as "bula-doota", "wee-arra", "wamba" and "woo-ra-ling" by the Aboriginals of Australia.

John Gould, who is also known as the "bird man", wrote in detail about the cockatiels. The scientific name *Psittacus novaehollandiae* was given by

Gmelin, a naturalist. This name refers to the old name of Australia, which was New Holland. The name was renewed soon after. The new name coined was *Psittacus hollandicus*. This name was coined by Dr. Robert Kerr and was published in the year 1792. The literal meaning of this name was "New Holland's parrot". This name is closer to the scientific name used for the bird currently.

In the year 1832, a change in the family of the bird was suggested. The name of the family was changed to *Nymphicus*. This name is derived from the mythological creature, the nymph. The nymph is a female spirit creature and a lesser goddess. The name implies "feminine" or "girlish" characteristics of the bird. The cockatiel has a slender and petite body that earned it this name.

According to mythology, nymphs were known to socialize with the gods and goddesses. The current scientific name of the cockatiel *Nymphicus hollandicus* when translated means "Nymph of New Holland".

Cockatiel timeline

Here is a brief timeline of the discovery and evolution of various mutations when the bird was bred in captivity.

- James Cook makes his way to Australia-1770
- Gemlin coins the name *Psittacus novaehollandiae*- 1788
- Kerr coins the name *Psittacus hollandicus* - 1792
- Wagler suggests the genus *Nymphicus*- 1832
- Cockatiels are taken to the Western World- 1845
- Cockatiels are showcased in Paris at the Jardin des Plantes- 1846
- Germany takes on captive breeding of Cockatiels and popularizes it as a hobby for the rich- 1850
- Cockatiels are bred at the London Zoo- 1863
- Australia imposes a ban on the export of native species-1894
- The first breeding pair is brought to the USA- 1910
- San Diego introduces the Pied variety increasing the popularity of the cockatiel- 1951
- Recessive silver variety is bred in Europe-1960s
- Pearl variety is bred in Germany- 1967
- Cinnamon variety is bred in Belgium- 1968
- Fallow variety is bred in Florida- 1971

- Whiteface variety is bred in Netherlands- 1976
- Yellowcheek, Platinum and Olive varieties are found in Germany, Australia and USA respectively- 1980s.
- Suffused variety is found in Australia- 1990s.
- Yellowface variety is found in Florida- 1996
- Pewter variety is found in Australia- 1998
- Australian Yellowface is discovered- 2001.

There are several new varieties that are being created. New mutations appear in different parts of the world thanks to the breeding efforts of seasoned cockatiel enthusiasts. The popularity of the bird grows with each new variety found. Of course the temperament added to the beautiful appearance makes it the perfect pet bird.

6. Range and Distribution

Cockatiels are distributed all over the world today since their captive breeding gained more momentum with the rise in popularity. Today, these birds cannot be exported from Australia, so the pets that you will find all over the world are the ones that have been bred in captivity.

The range of cockatiels

These birds are found all across the mainland of Australia. The populations are denser in the southwestern parts of the continent according to the animal diversity website of the University of Michigan. The tiny island of Tasmania, which is located to the south of the coast of Australia, also has some populations of these wild birds. It is believed that these wild populations were inadvertently transferred to this tiny island. Hence, they are not native to this region.

Nesting and migration

Cockatiels began to migrate when Australia was hit by dry spells for a long time. They continue to be migratory birds. However, the migration pattern of these birds are limited to their natural range. They are nomadic, but within the region that they are originally from. When the climate gets wetter in the Northern parts of Australia, these birds move constantly in search of fresh water and food. The birds that are native to the temperate parts of Australia, namely the southern region, tend to migrate in huge flocks. The temperature and climate in these zones are more predictable. The migratory pattern of the birds in this region varies as per the season.

Native habitat of the cockatiel

The Australian inland that consists of fresh water are favored by these birds over the Australian coastline. These birds are seldom found in areas with dense forests. They prefer to inhabit the savannas and woodlands. The acacia seed is the preferred food of these birds. Therefore, you will find these birds in large numbers in areas that have Acacia shrubs. The nests of the birds are built in the hollows of large trees. These nests are built at a height of about 3-6 feet above the ground. Nests are almost always found in areas with potable water.

Cockatiels play a very important role in the ecosystem of Australia. These birds are responsible for the dispersion of the seeds of native plants. Most often, these birds consume seeds that are sun-dried. However, they are also known to consume fresh fruits and seeds from time to time. The fact that these birds eat extremely messily works to the advantage of the Australian ecosystem. Because of the habit, these birds are capable of scattering seeds to almost 5 feet away from their nesting and roosting area. As a result, they have a positive influence on the Australian ecosystem.

7. Conservation Status

With the ban on the export of cockatiels from Australia, the wild populations have remained stable. This effort was primarily to safeguard the population of this bird that began to grown in popularity world over because of easy breeding in captivity. These birds also have the perfect qualities to be a great pet in any household.

Of course, they are bred in large numbers world over. Therefore these birds are categorized under Least Concern by the IUCN Red List of endangered species.

Chapter 2: Sourcing a Cockatiel

There have been several instances when people have brought home beautiful cockatiels. After spending some time with the bird and bonding with him, the bird suddenly develops illnesses and dies eventually. This is the most heartbreaking thing that can happen.

To avoid this, you need to make sure that you source your bird from the right people. Bringing a sick bird home is definitely a noble thing to do. However, it is recommended that you only venture into this when you have ample experience with parrots or cockatiels.

This chapter tells you all about the different sources that are available to you and how you can make the most of each one of them.

1. Buying from a breeder

Cockatiels are definitely among the easiest birds to breed. It is a no-brainer that there are several cockatiel breeders cropping up in all corners of the world. As a responsible pet owner, it is your job to make sure that you only encourage breeders who are genuinely interested in the well-being of the bird. There are many commercial breeders who use unethical breeding techniques to produce these birds in large quantities. This is almost like a puppy mill for birds.

Here, you are likely to get birds that are sick or poorly managed, leading to several behavioral issues. So, when you approach a breeder, make sure that he or she is reliable and is completely genuine. There are several things that you can check to make sure that you are going to the right breeder.

Is it a closed or open aviary?

There are two types of aviaries that are normally found. Closed aviaries are the most preferred type, as the birds raised in them are less prone to diseases and health issues. A good breeder will practice a closed aviary system, which has the following characteristics:

- Visitors are not allowed inside the aviary without a change of clothes and shoes. It is mandatory to wash your hands thoroughly before you enter the aviary.

- Birds from other aviaries or pet birds are not allowed inside these aviaries as a quarantining measure.

- You are not allowed in the aviary if you have been to any area which is likely to have parasites or diseases transmitted by other birds. This includes freshwater areas, parks and other places with wild birds.

- All birds are properly quarantined before being introduced into the aviary. More often than not, the birds in the aviary are the birds that are bred within the facility.

These measures ensure that the birds are not exposed to any potential carriers of diseases and infections. The area is also secured from other animals or predators who could carry parasites that will affect the birds. You are most likely to find birds that are healthy and in great condition in these closed aviary systems

What is the condition of the birds?

The condition of the bird and the space that they live in tells you what to expect from these birds when you take them home. If you see the following signs, make sure that you look for another breeder to buy your bird from:

- The cages are poorly managed. You will see feces stuck on the bars and also particles of the feces in the food and the water bowls.

- There are several feathers on the floor of the cage or aviary even when the birds are not really molting.

- The birds have feathers that are ruffled and unkempt. Cockatiels are known to be very clean birds that groom themselves quite well.

- You will see stale and rotting food in the cages. This means that the birds may have developed some food related infections that will manifest in the future.

- The cage is damp and dingy. This could mean several fungal infections that are fatal for birds.

- The eyes of the bird are cloudy. In healthy birds, the eyes are clear and free from any discharge or crusting.

- There is nasal discharge or discharge around the beak of the bird.

- The feathers near the tail are matted together. This is a sign of digestive disorders or infections in the birds.

- The birds stay close to the floor or in a corner and will not approach you when you get near the cage. Cockatiels are curious birds by nature. They will be inquisitive and approach you when they are healthy. Lethargy and inactivity is a sign of health issues in birds.

Is the breeder willing to answer questions?

A good breeder is very passionate about the species of bird that he or she is dealing with. If the breeder is only looking to make a sale to you, they may brush off questions and even avoid answering them. You can ask questions about the care and health requirements of the bird. You can even ask for testimonials and recommendations from previous clients of the breeder. If he/she is hesitant to share details, then it is a red flag that you need to watch out for.

A good breeder with enough knowledge about cockatiels can be invaluable in your journey with your bird. They will be able to answer several queries for you when you face issues along the way with your cockatiel. Make sure you read up a little about cockatiel care to ensure that you are getting the right answers to your questions.

Are the birds hand raised?

This is one of the most important questions that you should ask your breeder. A breeder who hand raises their birds is genuinely interested in their well-being. Of course, it also means that the birds are used to human interaction and will not shy away from you when you take them home.

Hand raised birds are easier to tame, so if you are a novice in the world of parrots, it is advisable to look for a breeder who hand raises the birds. If you have to start from scratch, you will need some experience with parrots or cockatiels.

2. Buying from a pet store

Pet stores are often chosen as the easiest source to get your cockatiels from. There are some pet stores that are genuine and invested in providing proper care for their animals.

However, there are several commercial ones that buy from breeders who mass-produce these birds using unethical measures. These are the pet stores that are only interested in making a sale. It is best that you avoid them as you will probably end up with a bird with several health issues.

How to look for a pet store

One of the reasons why people choose pet stores is the convenience factor. You will find more pet stores than breeders in your vicinity. If you are looking at buying from a pet store, it is not all bad. However, you need to make sure that you make the right choice.

Before you walk into a pet store, check their website and also ask for recommendations. There are several local bird clubs and even online forums that you can approach to get a list of the best pet stores in your locality. You can even contact dedicated cockatiel clubs where you will also meet several other cockatiel owners who can give you great advice on getting a bird who will fit into your home perfectly.

Another great way to look for pet stores is going online. You can look up directories to find a list of the best pet stores. The website of genuine pet stores will usually have pictures of the birds and animals that they are selling on their websites. You will also have testimonials from people who have bought their birds from these pet stores. If you have friends or neighbors who have pet birds, they can become the most reliable source to get information about local pet stores.

What to look for when you visit a pet store

Just like with a breeder, you can understand the philosophy of a pet store when you pay a visit to them. Here are some things that you should look for when you visit them:

- The staff should have knowledge about the cockatiel. They should be well informed about all the birds and animals that they are selling at their facility. You can ask them questions about the natural habitat, food habits and general care of the bird that you want to buy. You will have to have some prior knowledge to make sure that you are getting the right answers.

- The maintenance guidelines of the birds are the same as they are for breeders. The birds should look healthy, the cages should be clean and the birds should have a constant supply of clean food and water.

- The birds should be used to handling. In most pet stores, the birds and animals interact with several people on a daily basis. The pet store staff should be able to help you handle the bird that you want to buy. They should be able to give you tips and proper guidance with respect to handling a bird for the first time.

- Several species of birds and animals should not be placed in the same enclosure. This especially applies for predatory animals and prey animals. If they have been kept in the same space, chances are that the bird is extremely defensive. This leads to behavior such as dominance, nervousness and even some amount of aggression.
- If the bird is kept with several other birds in an aviary, make sure that you check the behavior of the bird. If the bird is too dominant, he may practice the same with you. If the bird is fearful and always secluded in a corner, you may have to deal with various behavioral issues.

- The pet store should practice proper quarantining methods before introducing new birds into their stores. This ensures that the existing birds are in good condition and free from any health issues.

- The pet store should have the necessary license to breed and sell the birds. This ensures that they are not involved in trafficking of birds of any species. Then, you can be assured that they are genuine and that they are following the rules and regulations correctly.

3. General guidelines for buying cockatiels

Whether you are buying from a breeder or a pet store, here are some guidelines that you need to make sure you are following:

- Never agree to a sale through an online advertisement or post. No matter how genuine it may seem, you can never be sure of any livestock that you purchase online. Only buy from an online store if you know of someone personally with experience buying from a breeder or vendor.

- If you choose to buy from a breeder who is located in another city or state, make sure you pay a visit at least once to check the facility. Learn about the transportation methods and the guarantee that is provided by them with respect to any issues that the bird may face during the transport.

- Avoid buying birds without a health guarantee. We will talk about a health guarantee in detail in the next section. However, it is important for you to know that a health guarantee is almost like a quality check for a breeder or a pet store. It ensures they are confident enough to give you a guarantee on the health of the bird after the sale is made.

4. What is a health guarantee/certificate?

Getting a health certificate for a pet bird is mandatory. This is a guarantee of sorts on the health and quality of the bird that you are bringing home. For cockatiels, a health guarantee is valid for a 90 day period. In that time, if the health of your bird deteriorates, the breeder will give you a replacement or will return your money. Any breeder who practices good husbandry will give you a health certificate by default. If he or she hesitates, you may want to reconsider your options.

Note: If you are ordering a bird online, you may not be able to avail a health certificate. This is because the health problems may be caused due to the shipping conditions that the breeder has no control over.

Here are a few conditions that you will see in any bird health certificate:

- The bird should be checked for any health issues within 72 hours of the purchase. Usually, you need to consult a vet recommended by the aviary. However, if you can find a breeder who lets you choose the vet, it is a better idea as you can be sure of no internal connections.

- If any illness is caused because of poor conditions that you keep the birds in, the health guarantee will not cover for it.

- Accidents are not covered by the health insurance. This includes any attack by your existing pets, fires, smoke, etc.

- No veterinarian costs will be covered by health insurance.

- Behavioral issues in the birds will not be covered in this insurance.

- In the case of some species, any incompatibility between the birds will be covered in this insurance if you are buying them in pairs. This is especially true when you are investing in a bird that is expensive.

When you get your birds examined, if the vet is able to determine the presence of any health condition that may be bacterial, viral or genetic, the breeder must give you a replacement.

For first time bird owners, it is a good idea to consult a friend who already owns a bird with respect to the conditions mentioned in the agreement. Normally, there are aviculturists who will offer this service at a small price. If you have no experience with cockatiels, this is a good option for you. They will not only be able to verify the terms and conditions but also the health of the bird that you are bringing home.

5. Second hand birds

You may have the opportunity of bringing home the pet from another home and becoming a foster parent. This may happen when someone decides to move and is unable to take their pet along with them. They may be unable to meet the demands of a bird due to personal or professional reasons. If this is the source that you are opting for, you may want to learn a few things first.

You can bring the bird home from a rescue home or from the home of a friend or family. Usually, any bird that has been abandoned by the owner will be sent off to a shelter. Now, when you choose this bird, you need to go into every detail of its history. This includes the caging practices, the history of the bird's relationship with the previous owner, the habits that the bird is used to such as having a blanket over the age, diet, sex, etc. The more you know, the more you can understand about the possible behavior of the bird. These experiences will have a very strong impact on the personality of the bird.

The first thing to know about a cockatiel that you are adopting is that you have keep your expectations really low. They may not form a bond with you instantly or may not form a bond at all. Remember that this bird has undergone the stress of changing homes, forming new bonds and in worst cases, abuse. This may be very annoying for someone who is expecting to have a loving bird that will play and cuddle. If you can prepare yourself to provide care for the bird despite possible behavioral issues, you can bring home a second hand bird. Otherwise, you may give up on the bird, adding to his existing stress and plight.

If you are planning to adopt a cockatiel, here are a few helpful tips for you:

- Make sure that you have some previous experience with respect to dealing with birds.

- You need to be able to understand the difference between a bird who is young and a bird who is mature. The former is likely to have a more volatile personality. They will respond to everything differently, including food.

- You must be willing to spend a certain amount of money on professional care for the bird. If you are a first-time owner, this is a must. Do not pretend to know anything about the bird if you really don't. That is in the best interest of your feathery friend.

- You need to be very patient and persistent. If you walk out on the bird, you will make his condition worse. Only if you are ready to deal with a challenge should you accept to adopt a bird.

On the bright side, with constant care, the behavioral issues of the bird will disappear with time if you are going to provide him or her with a loving home. The time that this will take is one thing that cannot be guaranteed. It is also possible that you may adopt a perfectly well-behaved bird with no signs of behavioral issues. It is harder when you bring home a bird that has formed a bond with the owner than when you bring home a bird that has been neglected or ill-treated. The latter is almost like a brand new bird that will adapt to your home in no time. The only thing you will have to do is love your bird with your heart and you will receive the same in return.

6. Adopting a cockatiel

Not everyone is equipped to take care of a pet bird. For this reason, and many more, people give cockatiels away to shelters almost every day. In some cases, these birds are rescued from homes that are abusive as well. You can approach a rescue shelter in order to adopt your pet cockatiel.

Of course, adoption is recommended for someone with some experience with birds. However, if you are willing to put in some effort into raising your bird, you will be able to manage a rescued bird even if you are a complete beginner.

This is one of the noblest ways to find your companion for life. Adoption is quite simple, as every organization has a set of rules and guidelines that you need to follow to bring home your pet bird. Here is a step by step guide to adopting a cockatiel.

When it comes to adoption, there are two options: you can either approach a rescue or you can approach a shelter. While they may seem like the same thing, they are quite different in reality.

Procedure for shelter adoption

A shelter is a facility that is run by the local government or by a non-profit organization. These are public facilities such as the pound and the animal control. Of course there are some private facilities as well. These are usually referred to as humane societies or clubs. They usually have more branches.

These shelters are either government funded or are run by individuals or a group of people. Shelters work like an organization and have dedicated staff and even fixed hours for working. These are also several volunteers who assist with adoption and general operations at these facilities.

You can look for sources to adopt your bird from online. There are dedicated websites that will give you details about the closest shelters to your home. They will also give you details on the birds that are available at these shelters.

With most of these shelters, the number of volunteers and staff is very low. That is why calling them to make enquiries may not be the best idea. Instead, you should visit them during their working hours. The details of the working hours are generally provided on the official website of each of these shelters. The websites will also list the birds that are up for adoption. If you can spot a cockatiel among the listing, the next thing to do is to visit the shelter.

The procedure for adoption varies from one shelter to the other. The overall process is quite similar however. Some rules that you need to be aware of before you adopt a pet bird:

- The first step is to find a bird that you would like to adopt. Go through the listings provided by the website of the shelter.

- Paying a visit to the shelter to see the bird is a must. There is usually a reception desk at each shelter where you can get all the details of the bird that you want. You can even interact with the bird for a while to understand the personality and the temperament of the bird in general.

- You may have to pay an adoption fee in some shelters. This fee ranges from $20-$100 or £5-£50. It is entirely dependent on the shelter that you plan to adopt from. Also, the more medical attention the bird may have needed after rescuing him, the higher the fees. This is primarily to ensure that any medical attention that is needed for the bird is covered.

- Once you have decided upon the bird that you want to take home, you will have to give them a valid ID. Shelters also have a mandatory house check. With exotic species like the cockatiel, illegal trading and breeding is always a threat. These house checks are mandatory to ensure that the bird is going into a good home. The goal is to prevent any chance of trauma if the bird needs to be rescued again and has to go through the whole process all over.

- You will have to complete the necessary paperwork. This will include details of vaccination and will also provide other health records of the bird.

- Make sure you spend some time with the bird before you decide to bring him or her home.

Procedure to adopt from rescue facility
The term rescue refers to an individual bird that has been rescued by someone and is currently under their care. These birds can also be cared for in a private boarding facility. Some facilities are run by volunteers and have regular adoption events.

When looking for listings for adoption, a rescue listing can be contacted immediately. If it is a private boarding set up, you will have to fill in applications and complete their adoption procedure.

Some rules that apply to rescues include:

- You can send an email or connect with the rescue using the contact details provided. Rescues are quick to respond and will call you immediately.

- You will have to provide all the necessary details about yourself. You can get all the details about the bird that you want to rescue through this conversation.

- When you are sure that you can handle the responsibility of the bird, you can visit the shelter or one of their adoption events.

- A home check is necessary when you adopt from a rescue. Only when the rescue is convinced that your house is a suitable environment for the bird will you be able to adopt.

- Once you have chosen to adopt the bird, you will have to submit all the necessary ID proof. You will be handed over the health reports of the bird as well.

- In case of an adoption contract, it has to be signed and the adoption fee should be paid. This fee is between $100-$300 or £50-£150.

What is the difference?
While the philosophy and the objective of rescues and shelters is to make sure that the birds get a good home, they differ quite greatly in the processes that they follow.

With a shelter, you have the option of looking at different birds before you make the final choice of which one you take home. Shelters have a more stringent process. However, some of them will let you take the bird home the day you approach them for adoption.

Adopting from a shelter is definitely a much cheaper option. However, medical expenses are higher in the case of a shelter.

When you adopt from a rescue, you have better access to all the information about the bird. The bird is also more cared for as it gets individual attention. However, with the adoption process you will see a lot more involvement from a rescue.

Since you are able to gather all the information that you need about the bird, it also means that you will find one that is more suited to your requirements. In the case of a rescue, the adoption fees are higher. However, you do not have to worry about veterinary costs with a rescue.

When you adopt a cockatiel, be prepared for certain behavioral issues that stem from the fact that the bird may have had a history of abuse or several illnesses. For adoption, it is always recommended that you have some experience dealing with cockatiels or some type of parrot.

7. Pros and Cons

Now that you know where to bring your pet cockatiel home from, it is also necessary to understand what to expect when you actually bring the bird home. While cockatiels are wonderful creatures, remember that there are two sides to every coin. Here is a list of pros and cons to help you decide if the cockatiel is the right bird for you or not.

Pros:
- Cockatiels are the perfect pet for an apartment because of their small size. If you have space constraints, then this is the perfect bird for you.

- These birds have a smaller appetite in comparison to other birds in this family. So, he will be a better option if you are looking for a pet bird on a budget.

- These birds are extremely fun. They will keep you entertained by making faces, puffing up their feathers all of a sudden, making weird noises with their beaks and a lot more. They are sure to bring a smile to your face every time you look at them.

- The poop of the cockatiel is much smaller than most other birds. This means that it is relatively easy to clean up after a cockatiel. All you need is a piece of tissue paper and it is easy to get rid of it all.

- With a cockatiel, you have a companion for life. These birds are great with people and get along perfectly. They are easy to train, are extremely calm and are happy for the most part. They are likely to develop a few behavioral issues when they approach puberty. Besides that, having a cockatiel is simply a hoot.

- Cockatiels are gentle birds which makes them safe to have around kids. Of course, you need to make sure that children are taught to handle the bird carefully without scaring or startling him too much.

- The cage requirements of the bird are easy to meet. Since you do not have to buy a massive cage, it is less expensive. You can also place the cage in your home easily as it will not take up as much space. Of course, the smaller the cage, the easier it is for you to clean.

- These birds are beautiful to look at. The feathers are extremely soft. This means that you will enjoy cuddling your bird. Whether your bird will appreciate the cuddling or not depends entirely on his or her personality. The way they preen their feathers is also a lot of fun to watch.

Cons:
- While the poop of the cockatiel is relatively smaller, you will have a hard time if you do not clean it up instantly. The poop of the cockatiel dries up almost instantly, leaving a crust that is very difficult to clean up. So make sure you wipe up after your bird in case he has an accident. Also keep the cage well lined to avoid spending hours scrubbing the floors.

- These birds are not as talkative as you would like a parrot to be. They will learn to mimic a few sounds and words but nothing more.

Therefore, if you are looking exclusively for a bird that can talk, then the cockatiel is probably not your best bet.

- Night frights is a common issue with cockatiels. This means that they wake up at odd hours screeching and flapping their wings about in a fit. A bird that has had a night fright is very difficult to calm down. This is something that you will have to deal with especially when the bird hits adolescence. You can learn with experience but in the initial period, the night frights can be terrifying.

- Cockatiels love to preen themselves, no doubt. They also tend to shake their feathers out regularly. While this is not really an issue, it can be one when you have someone in your home with allergies. The feather dander can cause serious allergic reactions and it is necessary for you to consult your doctor if you are aware of any such issues within your family.

The one thing that you need to keep in mind is that cockatiels are a lifelong commitment. They can live up to 30 years of age, which means that you need to plan well into the future before bringing one home. You also need to spend some time with your bird each day. Only when you are sure that you can make this commitment should you bring a cockatiel home.

With the right living conditions and care, cockatiels are an absolute delight to have as pets.

Chapter 3: Preparing your home for a cockatiel

Once the source for your cockatiel is fixed, you will need to make your home completely ready for the bird. Cockatiels are extremely hardy birds, so they are relatively easier to prepare for. However, there is some stress involved in the transition that the bird needs to make from the breeder's or the pet store to your home.

To make this transition easier on the bird, you need to keep some basics in place. It will also help you relax around the bird during its initial phase in your home instead of scrambling around.

1. Get the carrier cage ready

Before you bring your bird home, you need to make sure that you have the right medium to transport your bird. You must never get the bird home from a breeder's or a pet store in a cardboard box. These boxes are not stable enough to offer support to the bird during his ride home. There is also a risk of the bird escaping from the box, as it cannot be secured completely and effectively.

How to set up the transport cage

- It is a good idea to invest in a smaller cage to transport your bird. This will also be extremely useful in the future when you want to take the bird to the vet or when you want to travel with the bird. The cage should be large enough for the bird to spread his wings and should have ample headspace. With this cage, you need not worry about providing space for the bird to fly or move around.

- It is best that the cage is made of the same material as the housing area that you set up for the bird. We will discuss the options available in detail in the next chapter.

- Once you have purchased the cage, make sure that you line it with a good substrate. The best option for temporary enclosures is newspaper or shredded tissue paper. They are extremely easy to clean and are also quite absorbent.

- Place a water bottle in the cage instead of a bowl. This avoids any spilling of water, which can cause dampness and discomfort to the bird.

- Provide some roosting area in the cage that is covered. If you are using this transport cage to bring your bird home, you may want to provide him or her with some secure place to hide. You can cover a portion of the cage with a blanket or even place a sleeping tent that is commercially available.

- Place a few toys in the cage that the bird can chew. The bird may not really want to play with the toy, as he may be too terrified. It can also be an outlet for anxiety with most of the birds. If your breeder is willing to give you a toy from the aviary it is best, as it helps your bird feel more secure, as there is some familiarity with the toy.

When you drive the bird home
- The drive home is the most stressful part of the transition for the bird. The car is one of the most unnatural environments for a bird. The smell, the movement, the temperature and several other factors end up making it a source of great stress. It is also possible that the bird you are bringing home has never been in a car before. So, you need to keep a few things in mind to ensure that the bird is comfortable.

- Set the cage of the bird in a place where it is most secure. This could mean placing it on the backseat. Better still, have someone sit in the front seat and hold the cage. Of course, you will never put the cage in the trunk of the car.

- Keep the temperature slightly lower than room temperature. This avoids any issues related to overheating in the bird. You must also not keep the temperature too low as it may have an adverse effect on the bird's health.

- Make sure that the windows are fully closed. Drafts can be stressful to the bird. Leaving the window open also puts the bird at risk of escaping or getting injured while trying to. It is better to be safe than sorry.

- It is important that you do not talk to the bird when you are driving home. You may feel extremely excited and may want to start a conversation and befriend your little companion immediately. However, you need to also understand that the bird is already coping with a lot of new sounds and images. When you talk to him, it is an added sound for him to cope with. He also tries to register the image of your face, the expressions and more. With birds that are as intelligent as cockatiels, the need to analyze their environment thoroughly leads to a lot of stress. They need to be sure of any changes that may occur in their immediate environment. So, the fewer changes you introduce on the first day, the better it is for your bird.

- It is a no brainer that you will not play any loud music in your car when you are driving home. If you must play music, you can play soft, relaxing music that will soothe the bird.

- Keep an eye on the bird. If he sticks to one corner of the cage on the floor, it is normal. This is the response to any discomfort or fear in a bird. However, if the bird gets sick, you may want to take a few breaks every 20-30 minutes if your ride home is longer than that.

- If you are lucky, your bird may be absolutely comfortable with the ride home. He may look alert all the time and will also seem to really enjoy the ride home. Just make sure that you keep the environment free from any possible stressors.

2. Set up the housing area

There are a few rules that you need to follow when choosing the size of the cage that you want to keep your bird in. There is a value called the bird number to size ratio. In the case of cockatiels, you should be able to provide about 3-4 inches of floor space for every pair of birds that you want to house.

The height of the cage is not really important, as it does not really interfere in the personal space of each bird.

The ideal size for a cage for your cockatiels is 24" x 28" x 24" (length, depth and height). This should be able to accommodate one pair easily.

Here are some things you must not do when you are buying a cage for your cockatiel:

- Do not go for enclosures that are too decorative and intricate in design.

- Make sure that the cage does not have many crevices that will be difficult for you to clean in the future.

- Cylindrical cages should be avoided, particularly ones that are small in diameter.

- There should not be any gaps that may trap the feet of the birds.

- Watch out for paint that may peel off from the cage or from the perches or other items on the cage.
- Do not get any decorative items that use treated wood, as they may harm the bird.

You have the option of building your own flight cage in case you do not want to invest in large cages that can be very expensive.

Types of cockatiel cages

Building the enclosure on your own
There are various types of aviaries that you can build including outdoor aviaries or full wire aviaries. The designs and plans are easily available on the internet. However, you need to have some basic considerations before you actually construct an enclosure for your bird.

You can get a wire enclosure constructed for as little as $10 and this is the most economical option available. This can be a super fun project. All you will have to do is dedicate a little time towards it.

The best type of aviaries to build are the free standing ones and not the permanent ones. That way it is also easy if you decide to move. Now, the only thing you need to remember with any permanent structure is that you may have to get permissions from zoning departments in your area.

Here are a few things you must consider before you construct an enclosure for your birds:

- Make sure you find a good location that is free from any traffic and noise.

- You should have access to water and safe electrical outlets.

- If the enclosure is indoors, you need to make sure that you give the birds ample air flow in order to be healthy.

- Indoor enclosures should be built in a way that they are easy to clean.

- You need to make sure that an outdoor aviary has good drainage. This will ensure that there are no damp floors, which may lead to disease.

- In the case of outdoor aviaries, it is also important to ensure that the area is safe from any pests or predators.

- As discussed before, the enclosure should be longer and not taller. You need to be able to provide ample floor space to each bird. A simple measure of 4 sq.ft per pair should help you understand the size of the aviary.

- The cage door is the trickiest part of the enclosure. You need to make sure that it is easy to access while keeping the birds safe from any chance of escape.

After you have taken care of all these considerations, the next thing to do would be to make sure that you get the right material to construct the enclosure with. Here are a few tips to help you with that:

- You can get all the material that you require from any home development store.

- The material that you purchase should be safe and must be free from any toxins.

- It is best that you avoid the use of redwood, cedar and screen wood. Pressure-treated wood should also be avoided.

- Any material that corrodes such as brass or copper should be avoided.

- Zinc and lead may lead to heavy metal poisoning. These elements are usually found in the paints used to construct the cage.

- If you must use galvanized hardware cloth, make sure that it is washed with vinegar.

- Furniture polish and metal polish must be avoided at all costs when you make the enclosure.

- It is a great idea to get PVC powder coated wiring because of the ease of maintenance.

- Plastic netting is only suitable for indoor cages, as the outdoor ones will have rodents chewing into them in no time.

- Wiring should not have spacing more than ½" and less than ¼".

- Never use screens, as the nails of the bird will get caught in it, leading to serious injuries.

The only other rule that you must keep in mind is to make the cage as large as you can afford. That way, your birds will have a lovely permanent home that they can live for the rest of their lives in.

Positioning the housing area

The most important thing with the enclosure is where you position it. You need to keep the safety and comfort of the bird in mind at all times. One thing with birds is that they tend to get really nervous if you tower over them all the time. The best way to position these cages is such that the perches are above your own eye level.

If you have placed the enclosure indoors, it is a good idea to have the enclosure near a window that can give the birds natural light. You also need to have a shaded area in the enclosure that the birds can rest in.

You need to make sure that the settings of the cage mimic natural light as closely as possible. If you need to provide artificial lighting, it is best that you provide full spectrum light. You need to set these lights to a timer that switches it on at dawn and switches it off at dusk, basically matching sunrise and sunset. You will have to make seasonal adjustments to match the length of the day.

Lighting is the most important thing for your cockatiels, as it plays an important role in the hormone cycle of the birds. This influences breeding.

You can opt for fixtures that emit UV lights, as UV light plays an important role in Vitamin D production and also calcium absorption in birds. You have to make sure that the cage is dark at night. Opting for a dim light is also a good idea to prevent any episodes of night fright.

There is no need to cover your cage at night. It is has been discouraged by a lot of bird lovers and owners as it can reduce the amount of fresh air that your bird gets. This may also upset your bird's sleeping cycle, as they may not wake up with the rising sun.

You need to give your bird a living area that is suitable for him. You need to keep the following points in mind to ensure that your home is bird proofed properly:

- Do not keep any cleaning agents near the cage, as they may contain ammonia and Clorox fumes.

- The birds should be kept free from any chlorine fumes.

- Products that give out mists or fumes like air fresheners should not be placed near the cage.

- You should not have a combustion exhaust around the cage.

- Disinfectants containing pine oil should not be placed near the cage.

- Ironing boards, heat lamps and pots containing Teflon should be kept away from the cage. When these surfaces are heated, they release a gas that is harmful for birds.

- Do not spray suede or leather protectant near the cage.

- Smoking near the cage area must be strictly prohibited.

- Be careful and watchful about gas link leaks.

- Moth balls should never be placed near the cage.

- Scented candles may contain fumes that are poisonous for birds.

- Varnish and paint removers should be kept away from the bird.

- You also need to make sure that the cage door is closed whenever you leave the room.

- If you plan to let the birds out of the cage for long periods, it is essential that you do not have any fans or table fans around the area.

The area that you choose to house your birds in should not have temperature fluctuations. The kitchen is one such example. You should also make sure that the area is not accessible to your other pets and is also free from any toxic plants. You can get the birds acclimatized to any temperature that is comfortable for you. All you need to make sure is that it does not fluctuate too much.

If your birds are going to stay outdoors, shade is absolutely necessary. If you live in an area where the temperature fluctuates, the cage should be placed in an area that is protected from this fluctuation. The plants that are around your aviary should be non-toxic and bird friendly.

It is absolutely mandatory to keep free ranging birds away, as they may contaminate the food of your birds and also spread infectious diseases.

With these tips and ideas, you should be able to find the ideal space for your aviary. That way your birds are not only safe but are guaranteed to be happy in the area that they are going to spend the rest of their lives in.

Accessorizing the cage

Stimulating the bird and making sure that he gets ample exercise is one of your biggest responsibilities. The perches and accessories of the cage are essential not only for physical exercise but are also important for feeding the birds and giving them ample visual barrier if you have multiple birds in your aviary.

The type of perch that you choose plays a very important role. If you opt for dowel perches, you may face issues like lack of exercise, as the bird may not get proper footing. These perches force the birds to shift all their weight on to one foot. As a result, in case there is an outbreak of bumblefoot, it may get aggravated.

Dowel perches may be included but should not be the only perch in your cage. Opt for perches that are made from nontoxic hardwood and clean material.

If you are planning to get a branch for your cage, make sure that it is obtained from a tree that has not been sprayed with any pesticides. Wood rot and mold should also be considered when you are bringing wood from the outdoors. The best option is to purchase manzanita branches, which you will find in any pet store.

Although some people may tell you that sandpaper covered perches are good for your bird as it keeps the toenails short, you must never opt for this. It leads to foot infections and bruises.

You must also place the perches such that they are not directly above one another or directly above the food and water bowls. This prevents any chances of contamination due to droppings. Make sure that perches made of wood are replaced regularly as they become contaminated with time.

The next most important cage accessories are the food and water dishes. The only thing you need to remember is that these dishes should be very easy to clean. The best option for a cockatiel is a stainless steel cup. Metal containers with soldered ends should be strictly avoided, as they may lead to lead poisoning.

The water and food bowls should be placed away from one another to encourage exercise. If you notice that your bird is nesting in the cups instead of feeding from them, you will have to shift to a tube style feeder.

You will not need too many toys for your cockatiel. These birds are not so demanding in this department as compared to parrots. Adding a swing is a good idea as long as it does not get in the way for the bird's movements. It must also never strike the wall of the cage.

You may add other modes of entertainment in the cage including short strings tied to the roof of the cage. This string should not be made of small fibers and should not be too long, as it may entangle the bird. About 2 inches is a good length for the strings.

Cockatiels will also appreciate a place to roost in at night. A nest or a perch should do the trick. You can place it near the upper corners of the cage. If you make a roosting area with wood, avoid cedar and redwood or any other pressure treated wood. You can use shredded paper, coconut fiber or tissue paper. Remember that this roosting area will also encourage breeding.

The nesting or roosting area is not mandatory. However, if you have several birds in your aviary, getting sleeping tents for birds also gives them a good hiding area in case one or more of their cage mates become aggressive.

When it comes to accessories for cockatiels, less is more. You have to make sure that the area is not too crowded. Flight should be comfortable, as this the most preferred form of exercise as far as cockatiels are concerned. This is also the most effective way of exercise.

Keeping the cage clean
The bedding that you choose is an important part of hygiene. You need to make sure that whatever you choose is highly absorbent in nature. Some of the best options for cockatiel cages include paper towels, paper, newspaper, paper bags, butchers' paper or just about anything that absorbs well.

Every night before you turn the lights out, you need to make sure that you take the substrate out and replace all the soiled layers.

The cages and perches should be cleaned out every week with mild liquid dish soap. You can scrub them well to make sure that any dry feces is removed entirely.

Disinfecting the cage once a month is essential. A weak solution of bleach that is about 1 gallon of water with ¾ cup of bleach should do the trick.

This will get rid of all the organic substances including feces, food and feathers. You need to remove as much as you can manually before you apply this solution to the cage.

Remove the birds from the cage when it is being cleaned. It is a good idea to have a small transfer cage that they can be housed in on a temporary basis. Bleach may be used only when the area is well ventilated. You should not use this solution on any metallic surface.

The cage should be dried before your birds are allowed into it. The birds must not come into contact with bleaching powder at any cost. You need to rinse the cage well and dry it in the sun before the birds are replaced.

Physical cleaning of the cage on a regular basis is one of the best ways to prevent diseases amongst your flock. One risk factor for the owners of birds is the inhalation of fecal dust and spores while cleaning the cage. This may aggravate existing respiratory problems.

The best thing to do would be to install an electrostatic type filter for the air. If your bird area has a central air system, you can prevent the transfer of pathogens.

Of course, all the food and water dishes must be cleaned everyday. If you see any food in the bowls, you need to discard it and make sure that your birds get fresh food every single day. That will keep them healthy and will prevent the chances of any fungal or bacterial growth inside the enclosure.

3. Bird-proof your home

While it may seem like your house is a safe haven for your pet bird, there are several things that can actually harm him. What seems like a regular household item can be hazardous to your cockatiel. There are also several chances that your bird may escape from your home into the outdoors. To prevent any accidents, bird-proofing your home is highly recommended. Here are a few tips to make your home safe for your cockatiel:

- Ensure that your bird is away from any poisonous foods like cocoa, avocado, chocolate, pits of fruits or any food that is high in sugar. You also need to keep the food of your bird free from any molding.

- PTFE or Polytetrafluoroethylene products such as Teflon can be extremely hazardous for your bird. These products are used in common household items like non-stick pots and pans. They release an odorless gas whenever they are overheated. This is poisonous for your bird. Check the labels on any utensil or ensure that the cage of the bird is away from the kitchen.

- Fumes released by the debris in self-cleaning ovens are also toxic for your bird.

- In general, objects that release any smoke or fume can be very dangerous for your bird. This is why your cockatiel should be kept completely out of bounds from your kitchen.

- Make sure that all the metallic material that is used in the construction of your cage is safe for the bird. Cages should have paint that is non-toxic. Spacing between the bars should be appropriate to prevent any choking or to keep the feet from getting trapped. There should not be any sharp edges in the cages either. This can cause gashes and injuries on the bird's body.

- If the bird has any leg bands, it is a good idea to replace them with microchips. Leg bands can lead to the loss of feet, toes and can even be fatal in very extreme cases. Have the leg band removed by the vet and replace it with safer identification methods.

- Avoid giving your bird food in any ceramic crockery. It may contain some traces of toxic metal. Instead you may give your bird food in specially made steel bowls or in glass bowls. The former is safer as there are no chances of it breaking and hurting the bird.

- Be cautious if you have any halogen fixtures in your home. These fixtures can become extremely hot. This leads to fatal injuries and even burns in case the bird accidentally comes into contact with it.

- Make sure that you do not use walnut shell or corn cob litter as substrate in the cage. It can be fatal for the bird if ingested accidentally. They are hazardous, as they are prone to hosting spores of fungus when they ferment. They have a certain moisture content that makes them more prone to this. It is best to use newspaper as substrate.

- Any metal component such as keys, paint containing metal, lead clappers, etc. should be kept away from the bird at all costs. Zinc and lead poisoning is always fatal for cockatiels.

- Transparent or reflective surfaces such as mirrors, glass doors and windows should be introduced to the bird. Make sure that your bird is familiar with their placement. It is also a good idea to use markers or decal to help your bird see the surface. This prevents them from crashing into them and getting injured.

- Always make sure that the ceiling fans are turned off if your bird is able to fly. Clipping the wings is a good idea if you intend to let the bird out of the cage.

- The other hazards in your home include hot pots, sinks, toilets, open windows and doors and poisonous plants.

- When you have any household plants, it is best that you keep the bird away from them. You may want to check if a certain plant is poisonous for a cockatiel or not before you bring it home. Some plants like azalea, daffodils, sago palm and asparagus can be hazardous to most birds. The chemical fertilizers that you use can also be dangerous. Use natural manure as much as possible.

- Never smoke near the cage of your cockatiel. Even the smallest traces of nicotine can be very dangerous for your bird.

- Essential oils and potpourri oils should be kept away from birds. Air fresheners, perfumes and aerosol sprays should also be avoided around the bird's enclosure.

- If you use candles at home, make sure you only use unscented ones. The ones that have some scent can release many toxins.

- Do not use any disinfectant, glue, carpet powder or paint around the enclosure of the bird. Even when cleaning the cage of your bird, make sure that you only use disinfectants that are approved by a vet and completely safe for your bird.

- The cage should be kept away from the air conditioning or heating vents. Sudden fluctuations in temperature can be fatal to birds. You also need to make sure that the cage of the bird is well ventilated. Any carbon monoxide accumulation in the cage is extremely dangerous. Just like humans, birds suffer from respiratory issues when they inhale carbon monoxide.

- Do not use any insect controllers or repellents near the cage of the bird. They contain components that can be carcinogenic. You also find the same components in some toilet cleaners and floor cleaners.

With these safety precautions, you will improve the living conditions of your bird. You will also be able to keep your bird safe and free from any accidents.

4. Make sure your family is prepared

In order to make the transition of your bird stress-free, it is not enough for you to understand what your bird needs. Every member of your family should be prepared for the arrival of the bird. This avoids any chances of unpleasant incidents with the new bird. The way you handle the bird, interact with him and maintain the ambience for the first few days plays an important role in the bird's well-being.

Here are some instructions that you should give all your family members before you bring the bird home:

- There will be minimal interaction with the bird. Cockatiels are extremely beautiful birds, so it is natural for your family members to want to touch and handle the bird. This should be avoided until the bird settles in. You must make sure that they do not even speak to the bird for the first few days.

- There will be no visitors until the bird is completely comfortable. Too many new faces and voices can lead to a lot of stress in the bird. If you are planning parties and get-togethers, make sure you put it off until your new bird begins to look calmer and more composed in his new environment.

- You will not play any loud music or keep the television on at high volumes near the bird. This can disturb the bird and lead to health issues related to extreme stress.

- If you have children in the house, make sure that you tell them not to tease the bird. The cockatiel is generally a very calm bird. However, when startled or approached roughly, they may nip as a means of self-defense. Cockatiels are large enough to cause serious injuries to children.

- Another family member besides the one who has brought the bird home should have access to any emergency number. This includes the number of the veterinarian, breeder or any other animal helpline that you may have to contact in case of an emergency.

Work together as the new bird's flock to make him feel more comfortable. The more you work towards improving the bird's experiences for the first few days, the more likely he is to form a bond that is entirely trusting.

Chapter 4: The cockatiel and his new home

Once you have figured out how the cockatiel will be transported to the new home, the next step is to ensure that he is introduced to the new environment correctly. There should be no stress that is caused to the bird when he comes into your home.

This chapter will tell you all that you need to know about the first few days of your bird's arrival. The goal is to make sure that the cockatiel does not feel too overwhelmed. Make the transition gradual and you will have your bird's complete trust.

1. Getting him into the new cage

This is possibly the hardest part about making the transition. Unless the bird is hand raised and very accustomed to human touch, it is not the best idea to pick him up and put him in the cage.

Since he is already afraid of being put in a new space, he may resort to some nipping as a defense mechanism. This will spoil your bird's first interaction with you in the new space. It will become harder for you to gain his trust once this happens.

Instead, it is a good idea to let the bird take his time to get familiar with the sights and sounds of the new home. Just leave his cage in the room for some time and leave him alone. Birds have a way of exploring their space through sights, sounds and scents.

Then, you can just place the door of the carrier in front of the door of the housing area and let them stay open. Make sure you have an eye on the bird when you are doing this. You do not want him to fly away or have any accident. At this time, it is also essential to keep doors, windows and other escape routes shut.

The bird may take some time or may hop right into the new housing area. If you feel like the bird is taking too long, you can coax him with the help of a treat. Place a few seeds that all cockatiels are sure to get lured by in the new housing area.

When he walks in to grab the treat, gently shut the door of the housing area. Through this whole process make sure that you never force the bird to enter his new enclosure by shoving or even a gentle push.

You must also keep verbal communication minimal. Whistling "here birdy" etc. will only startle your bird and make the process slower. Let the bird get a feel of the space and then venture into new territories.

The lesser the bird feels threatened, the easier it will be for you to break the ice with the bird over the next few days. The initial experiences of the bird in your home are crucial in determining how your interactions in the future will be. If you scare him in the first few days, you may have a harder time getting him to trust you and form a bond with you.

Additional tips
The placement of the cage plays a very important role in helping the bird feel more comfortable. Here are some simple tips that you can follow when it comes to cage placement:

- Make sure that it is in a place that is quiet but still adjacent to all the activities of the family. The bird should be able to see you and your family but should not be in the middle of any commotion.

- The cage should be rested against something to make the bird feel comfortable. The best option is to keep the cage against a wall. That way the bird will never be caught off guard and will not have to worry about someone creeping up on him.

- The bird should not be in for any surprises. That means, any large furniture that may block your bird's view of your home should be accounted for.

- The bird should get enough sunlight but not direct sunlight. Make sure that the cage is not directly in front of a window. This make overheat the bird.

- If the cage is near the window, however, it is a great way for your bird to stay entertained.

- The kitchen is the worst place for a bird cage. The bird may be exposed to several fumes as well as smoke that can be fatal. The fumes from non-stick cookware especially can be very dangerous.

- You do not have to worry about getting your bird many toys on the first day. In fact, if you are bringing the bird home from the breeder, you may want to take an old toy back to help your bird have some sort of familiarity in the new home.

- Line the cage with enough substrate. On the first day, it is likely that your bird may poop several times, making the cage dirty. This is primarily because of the anxiety of being in a new place.

2. To interact or not to interact?

This is one of the biggest dilemmas that new owners face. How much interaction is too much? On the first day it is natural to want to spend as much time with the bird as possible. A pet always leads to a lot of excitement in the household.

However, the truth is that the lesser you interact, the happier your bird will be. There are some things that you can do to help the bird settle in and feel relaxed despite the stress of transition.

Remember, stress can lead to several health issues in birds. The first response of the bird's body to stress is a compromised immune system. So, it not only leads to possible behavioral issues but can also make your bird very sick. For the first few days, follow these simple tips to make your interactions with your bird more positive.

Even though cockatiels are small birds, you need to ensure that their cage is not too crammed and small. To make your cockatiel feel completely at home, you need to keep some food available to the bird as soon as it is in your home. You can provide the bird with the same food as the breeders and the pet store. Even if your bird is primarily on a seed diet, you should not make any changes on the first day. Also keep a dish of water ready, although cockatiels are known for going on for days without any water.

If you already have a few birds at home, make sure that your new bird is kept away from them for health reasons. Quarantining is a must. We will learn in depth about this in the following section.

Cockatiels are naturally very timid birds and tend to be quite shy as well. If you give them too much stimulus, it may really scare them and turn out to be hazardous. Let the birds take their time to settle in. If your bird seems too quiet and nervous, let him be.

Cockatiels will only become active when they are comfortable with their new environment. Until then, you need to make sure that the area that they are in is calm and quiet. The interactions at this point should happen at face level. Never tower over the bird, as they will begin to view you as a predator and will take a lot more time to trust you.

Choosing an outdoor aviary for cockatiels is not the best idea in the beginning. They will be too overwhelmed. Make sure that you house your birds inside your home. The way you house your bird also plays a big role in how your bird will respond to you.

The rule of thumb is that you need to keep your distance from your bird for at least 72 hours after he arrives. While this does not mean that you should avoid the bird completely, it does mean that it is not yet time to show your bird off.

Make sure that no strangers interact with the bird during that time. Loud music, partying and too much commotion should be avoided entirely.

When you do interact with your new bird, make sure that you are extremely gentle. You can only whisper to your bird and treat the bird like you really respect him.

There are several things you can do at this time to keep your bird engaged. Reading the newspaper, singing out songs softly and just talking to him about your day can be of great help. Make sure you maintain eye contact with your bird throughout. This helps them gain more trust on you and will ease the process of settling in.

Physical contact at this point should be avoided completely, even if your birds have been hand reared. Make sure that you only change the food, liner and the water in the cage. This should also be done very calmly and slowly. Every move should be deliberate and minimal in interaction.

The bird may move away from you, may show signs of aggression or may seem to actually run for cover when he sees you. This does not mean that your bird dislikes you. It is only an indication that he is trying to gauge and understand you.

With each day, you will see that your bird gets more and more comfortable around you. You need to stay persistent in your interactions in order to win him over.

3. The importance of quarantining

Quarantining is one of the most important practices if you have other birds at home. The reason for this is that most birds turn out to be carriers of deadly diseases. However, they may not show the signs of illnesses immediately. The incubation period for most microorganisms that affect birds is between 30-60 days. So it is recommended that you at least quarantine your new bird for 30 days before introducing him to the flock.

This helps you ensure that the bird is not carrying any infectious diseases. It keeps the whole flock healthy and prevents the outbreak of diseases among them.

Here are some quarantining tips that you should follow:

- Place the bird in an entirely different room for the first 30 days at least. This is the best option available. However, if that is not an option, make sure that the bird is in a separate housing area that is as far from the rest of your flock as possible.

- When you are feeding your birds, make sure that you feed the existing flock first and then move on to the new bird.

- Your hands should be washed thoroughly before you interact with the two separate housing areas. This includes cleaning, feeding and even handling your birds.

- It is a good idea to change your clothes and shoes before you meet your existing flock if you have interacted with the new bird.

Make sure that you follow these steps with your entire family. You want to make sure that you do not allow the slightest chance of infection. The problem with birds is that diseases manifest suddenly, so when you see the signs, the bird is already in the last stages of the disease. With most of the avian diseases, there is no cure, as the microorganisms are extremely potent.

A word of advice is that you make sure that anyone who may have been around birds washes their hands and feet thoroughly before interacting with your birds at any given time. For instance, if a friend has come to meet your bird after a stroll in the park and has perhaps stopped to feed ducks or pigeons, they must clean up.

This rule also applies to friends who have pet birds in their homes. This ensures complete safety of your flock at all times.

4. Introducing cockatiels to other birds

Cockatiels are generally extremely friendly and timid. However, with birds there is always a hierarchy that is established within the flock. Some birds are inherently dominant while the others are submissive. Unless you know this hierarchy, making sudden introductions can be dangerous. It can lead to quarrels and fights to establish the pecking order, which in turn leads to severe injuries.

- After quarantining, you can bring the cage of the new bird into the same room as the other birds.

- If the other birds are larger birds, it is best that you do not house them in the same enclosure.

- If they are cockatiels or sparrows, you will have to observe the birds well before you place them together.

- Once you keep the cages in the same room, observe the reaction of the other birds. Do they become irritable and aggressive? If yes, you may consider keeping them in separate enclosures. However, if the other birds merely respond to the calls of the new bird, which will make the noisier than usual, it may not be such a bad idea to introduce your birds.

- You can introduce the birds by putting them in a neutral enclosure. That way, neither bird is territorial and aggressive.

- Individual interactions starting with the least aggressive bird is the best option.

- Once all the birds in your aviary have been introduced to one another, you can try to place your new cockatiels in the mixed aviary too. Even the slightest sign of aggression means that you need to get your new bird out and house him separately.

- There are a few things that will help you decide if certain birds will be compatible or not.

- First, you need to understand the habitat of the bird. Birds that are comfortable feeding off the floor of the aviary will usually be less aggressive.

- On the other hand, if the bird species has special requirements with respect to the feeding area, the nesting spot, etc., they are aggressive.

- These birds tend to hijack the nesting areas of other birds, leading to a lot of confrontations and aggression among one another.

- When you house mixed birds in one cage, you are creating a colony. So, always ask your vet or breeder if a certain species is a colony bird or not.

- Even with successfully colonized birds, making sure that they get their individual space is mandatory.

- This means that each bird should have at least 2 cubic meters to himself.

- They also need to have their own perches and toys and also feeding containers that are easy to access and use. That way, you will have a peaceful colony of birds.

5. Introducing cockatiels to other pets

Every pet owner dreams about having a home where all the pets live in complete harmony. This wish is not completely outrageous. However, remember that your other pets such as the dog or the cat are predators by natural order. Birds, on the other hand, are prey animals. So, you need to be very cautious when you are making introductions.

The cockatiel is a small bird and even the gentlest nip or scratch from your dog or cat can have severe consequences. In fact, the saliva of cats is known to be very poisonous for birds. It is a good idea to take it slow and see how the animals react to each other before forcing introductions.

- Place the cage of your bird in a room where your pets will most often hang around.

- Watch the reaction of your pet. If they are very curious or excited at the sight of the bird, it is not time to let the bird out yet. In this excitement, your pet may accidentally harm the bird. The pet may only be trying to figure out who this new entrant in your home is.

- All you need to do is leave the cage there as long as your pets lose interest in the bird. They should not react to the bird's presence in your home.

- If you see that your pet is trying to perch on the cage or climb on it, discourage the behavior immediately. A sharp "No!" from your end should do the trick. This will lead to submissive behavior from your parrot when you do let him out of the cage eventually.

- When your cat or dog loses interest in the cage being in the room, let the bird out. Of course, you must only do this after you have trained the bird to step up and then go back into his cage. If not, you may not be able to get your bird away if your cat or dog decides to chase it around.

- Let them be for a while and see how your pet reacts. If you hear the slightest growl or see any discomfort in the pet's body language, get the bird away immediately.

You can try this a few times. If you see any negative behavior of your pet towards the bird, it is best that you keep the bird in the cage whenever your pet is around. It is in the nature of some pets to dislike birds.

You also have a problem on your hands if your pet likes the bird. A dog will place a sloppy lick on the bird if he grows fond of him. The cat may do the same. Remember that the saliva of your cat or dog is toxic for the bird.

Although you must familiarize your pet with your new bird, it is a good idea to never leave them alone at home unsupervised. If you do this, the animals must be in an enclosure. Otherwise, you may come home to some unintentional but unpleasant scene.

Chapter 5: Cockatiel Care and Bonding

Taking good care of your bird is your primary responsibility. You need to provide a good housing area. In addition to this, the birds should have good access to clean drinking water and food all the time.

Bonding with your bird is just as important for your cockatiel. They are birds who can keep themselves entertained, no doubt. However, they need to interact with their flock in order to stay mentally stimulated and happy in the environment that they are in.

When you are establishing a bond with your bird, you can try out several activities that are actually a lot of fun. To begin with, training your bird can be extremely satisfying. Once you have achieved the results that you want, the possibilities are endless. You can have your bird accompany you for any activity or even simple chores around the house.

1.What do cockatiels eat?
The secret to good cockatiel nutrition is variety. You need to give them different sources of nutrients and not just stick to pellets. Pellets are the easiest option, of course, but they do not give your bird too many benefits in the long run.

What cockatiels eat in the wild
In the wild, a cockatiel's diet is quite varied. They eat grass seeds mostly as they inhabit the arid regions of Australia. However, their diet also includes berries, fruits and vegetation in the surrounding areas. Occasionally, cockatiels are also seen raiding agricultural farms for corn and other such foods.

What you need to know about pellets
The first thing that you need to give your cockatiel is dry pellets. Choose natural pellets from brands like Zupreem or Harrisons. If you choose the former, it can make up for 30% of your bird's diet but if you choose the latter, it should not be more than 10% of your bird's diet. The rest of it should contain fruits and veggies along with treats.

Avoid colored or dyed pellets, as they may harm the bird. Pellets are made from crushed seeds and are full of fiber. They include a lot of vitamins and minerals such as calcium along with fruits and vegetables. These are all essentials in your cockatiel's diet. You can start the day out with these pellets and actually make them the base of the diet. You can give a cockatiel about 2 tablespoons of dry pellets a day.

Pellets are best stored frozen. Brands like Zupreem may spoil easily and need to be frozen. Pellets contain several nutrients and are hence a lot better for your bird than an all seed diet. Only seeds can cause health issues in the bird. Give your cockatiel fresh pellets every morning. Remove the leftovers and refill the food bowl every day.

Adding seed treats in between the pellets is a great idea and necessary for your bird's diet. You get seed treats like nutriberries that will add a lot of minerals and vitamins to the cockatiel's diet. Ideally birds as small as the cockatiel will consume about 2 to 4 of these a day. You can give them in between meals, ideally when they are half done with the pellets and once the pellets are fully done. There are other such treats as well that birds may like and you should be able to find them in any store.

Giving your bird fresh produce
Fresh food is a must for birds to thrive. Fruit and vegetables make up a large portion of cockatiel food in the wild. Therefore, it is essential that you include it in their regular diet as well.

Remember, fruits and vegetables provide the best source of minerals and vitamins for the birds. These foods are also lower in fat, making them the most suited option for your pet.

In addition to all of this, birds tend to adore the idea of eating fruit and vegetables because of the color of these foods. Each bird will pick his favorite fruit or vegetable. You will be able to understand this by offering all options and seeing which one excites your bird the most.

Make sure you provide your bird with organic produce. That way, you can be sure of minimal pesticide usage. You must also wash the fruit and vegetables thoroughly before giving them to your bird. Some bird owners suggest that you warm the fruit and vegetables slightly in order to make it easy for your bird to digest them.

You can provide almost all fruit and vegetables to your bird. However, you must avoid avocado at all times, as it is toxic. It is also a good idea to avoid iceberg lettuce. Although it does not really cause any harm, it is of no nutritional value to your bird.

The best choice of fruits and vegetables include:

- Bell peppers
- Beets
- Apples
- Broccoli
- Butternut squash
- Cilantro
- Collard greens
- Carrots
- Dandelion greens
- Corn on the cob
- Mangoes
- Mustard greens
- Pumpkin
- Papaya
- Peaches
- Sweet potatoes
- Spinach
- Zucchini
- Tomatoes.

Whenever possible, give your bird fresh food. Frozen vegetables may be given occasionally, however these fruits and veggies do not provide as much nutrition as fresh produce.

All fruits and vegetables that are large in size must be chopped well or grated before giving the bird any. As for leafy greens, leave them whole, as your bird will love to pluck out pieces using his beak. This is a wonderful stimulation activity for your bird

Bird seeds
You have a host of different types of bird seeds that you can get. The best type of seeds to buy, if you choose to feed your birdseeds, is the premixed variety. If you are experienced with birds you can, of course, make your

own mix. That way you can customize it as per the requirements of your birds.

In case you opt for a premixed seed bag, it is a good idea to pick up the special cockatiel bags. That ensures that the seeds aren't too large for your bird.

Seeds should always be fresh. You should make sure that there are no droppings of rodents or cobwebs in your seed bag. Bugs and larvae are the main issue when it comes to birdseed.

The best way to judge is to smell the bag of seeds. In case it smells rancid, discard it right away. You can also apply a simple towel test to the seeds. You can fold a spoonful of seeds in paper and moisten it a little. In the case of fresh seeds, they will sprout. If the seeds are stale or dead, you will not see any signs of sprouts.

Millet spray is a type of seed that your cockatiels will simply adore. The seeds are still present on the stalk and it is a great pastime for the birds to pull these seeds out and eat them up.

It is best that you reserve seeds for treats, especially millet spray. They do not have as much nutritional value as the other foods available for birds.

Importance of calcium in your bird's diet
Calcium is one of the most important minerals for your bird. Sometimes, your avian vet may recommend some supplements. Until such a time, try to find natural sources of calcium for your bird. Pellets are the best option for a steady calcium source, as most of them are fortified. You also get calcium perches and toys that the bird can enjoy and get his nutrients from.

Now just like us humans, birds need vitamin D in order to synthesize the calcium. All cockatiels need full spectrum sunlight, so you need to take them out at least once a day for good sunlight. You can take the cage out if possible. If not, you get special transparent cages without filters that are safer and easier to use. If possible, place the cage near a good enough source of sunlight for everyday access. It shouldn't be too bright or hot, however.

What not to feed your cockatiel

- **Peanuts:** While other nuts like hazelnuts can be great for the cockatiel, as they are a source of high protein, peanuts can cause health problems because of fungal toxins.

- **Onions and garlic:** These two should not be offered in any form to the cockatiels, as they cause some irritation to begin with. In addition to that, they can make your cockatiel very anemic.

- **Tomatoes:** Tomatoes, especially raw ones, are hazardous to birds as they are acidic vegetables. They potentially cause ulcers in cockatiels.

- **Mushrooms:** They can cause serious digestive issues and even liver failure in cockatiels.

- **Celery:** If you can remove all the stringy parts of celery, it is quite safe to feed to your cockatiel. If not, it may lead to crop impaction.

- **Avocados:** Avocadoes are poisonous for parrots in general. They contain a certain toxin called perrsin that can cause breathing difficulties or even kill your cockatiel in worst cases.

When you are uncertain of a certain food, be sure that you consult your vet or fellow cockatiel owners. When you are sure that it is of no harm to your bird, you can introduce the birds to it.

2. Keeping your bird clean

Good sanitation is extremely important for your bird's health. To begin with, your bird should be maintained well to avoid matting of the feathers and even infections because of dirt and debris.

These grooming activities are also crucial for the bond that you build with your bird. Grooming is a very natural behavior in the wild. It is often associated with mating. However, when you are around the bird and you handle him or her on a regular basis, you will notice that the bird gets more comfortable with you.

This also builds a sense of trust in the bird because he knows that you do not mean any harm. While cockatiels are known to keep themselves clean for the most part, some grooming options that you can try out are as follows:

Bathing your cockatiel
In general, cockatiels like to stay clean. They have several instinctive cleaning methods in the wild. You need to be able to provide the one factor that the birds miss, which is rain, through a regular bath. Now, as you know, cockatiels are from tropical parts of the world where rainfall is common. So, that is essential for them to stay clean. Besides that, they have natural ways of keeping their bodies free from any dirt:

Powdering down: This refers to a small amount of dander or powder that the birds produce from the feathers. All cockatiels have certain down feathers that continue to grow for long periods of time. These feathers have very fine extensions that break often. This powder coats the feathers and the body of the bird. This powder repels water and dirt. It sticks to the dirt and when the bird preens itself, falls down with the dirt. The more dander the bird produces, the healthier he will be. Of course this is not a welcome instinct for most pet cockatiels.

Preening: This is the healthiest natural grooming method for the birds. It is useful to scape feathers and keep them moist. You will see your cockatiel use the water from the bowls to preen himself. Besides that, preening ensures that all the feathers of the bird are in place and can be used properly. In the wild, parrots of any kind will not let one feather go out of place because it makes them more vulnerable to predator attacks. A feather sticking out means that the predator will be able to spot the bird in a flock.

When they preen themselves, these birds also break a certain gland known as the Preen gland or the Uropygial gland that is present just at the base of the tail. This gland produces a certain oil that the birds rub all over their feathers just to make them waterproof.

Bathing the cockatiel at home
If this is the first time your cockatiel is taking a bath in your home, you need to make it a pleasant memory for him. Sometimes, when they have been bathed very harshly in their younger days at the breeders' or at the pet store, they will develop a negative feeling towards bathing. They may scream and rant when they hear the sound of a water tub filling up.

In order to give your cockatiel a bath, just fill up a small bird bath or even sink with water and lead the bird to it. You can use toys or treats to do this. Allow them to stand at the edge of the sink and just explore. They may be excited but scared to get into the water.

In order to lower the cockatiel into the tub, allow them to perch on your palm and slowly lower him towards the water. Then let the bird step in. In about ten seconds of entering the water tub, the bird should become familiar with or just used to it. Keep talking to your bird and make him feel safe. Praise him when he is wading in the water. You can also put some of his favorite toys into the water.

If you need to use soap, it is safe to use any mild human soap or shampoo. However, it is recommended that you buy specially made soaps to avoid any sort of allergy or infection. You can make a diluted soap solution and use your hands to give him a lather. Take a lot of care to avoid getting any into his eyes. In case of thick dirt, you can use a washcloth or a very soft toothbrush to gently brush it off. Then rinse the bird well with clean warm water and use a towel to pat him dry.

Some cockatiel owners use hair dryers to dry their birds, but it is recommended that you let the bird dry naturally, as this gives them a chance to even preen their feathers into place. Of course you need to make sure that the air-conditioning and the fans are off in the room where the bird is drying himself off.

For fully-grown cockatiels, a bath is not necessary. You can simply spray some water on them or just allow them to walk around under the shower. You will get special shower perches in any pet store that allow you to place the perch on the tiles of the shower wall with suction cups. Avoid using soaps during showers, as your bird may not allow you to get it all off. They will only stay under the shower for a few minutes and fly off. This is just to make up for their instinctive love of the rain.

You can give your bird a thorough bath every fortnight. A light shower is recommended twice a week to keep the bird healthy and free from any infections. When you are putting them in a birdbath, make sure that it is very shallow, as parrots are not good swimmers as a general rule. It should just be enough for the bird to soak himself.

Nail and beak trimming

This grooming process is optional. If you notice that your bird's toes and beak are getting stuck in toys or any fabric, you can trim them to avoid any accidents. If the beak or toe of your bird is stuck to the fabric on your upholstery and he tries to move suddenly, there are chances that the whole toe is ripped off or the beak is severely damaged. To avoid this, trim the sharp ends.

Wrap the bird in a towel, only exposing the part that you want to trim. In the case of the beak, gently lift the upper mandible with your finger and feel the sharp end. Keep the beak supported and trim the beak using a nail file. When you feel that it is blunt, stop trimming. If the nail or the toe is too short, the bird will be unable to climb and hold properly.

Even with the toe, make sure that you have a finger supporting the nail you want to trim to avoid any chances of breakage or unwanted damage.

It is a good idea to give your bird perches and toys of different textures. That will let the nails and the beak stay blunt naturally. As the bird climbs or chews with the proper toys, the beak and nails get trimmed. You will see them rubbing their beak onto rough surfaces in an attempt to keep them trimmed. This is an instinctive practice that should be encouraged.

Remember that bonding with birds as intelligent as these requires a lot of effort from your end. These birds will analyze every situation that they are put into and even the slightest doubt will break their trust. If you have adopted a bird that has been abused, this will take longer. You will also need a lot of assistance from your avian vet to gain the trust of such birds. Take it one step at a time and make sure that you do not rush him.

Wing clipping

Some people believe that wing clipping is not ethically correct. If you are one of them, make sure that your home is a safe haven for your bird. You do not want to have any flight-related accidents at home. This may also lead to the escape and loss of your precious cockatiel.

If you have pets at home, do not clip the wings. This is your bird's only form of defense. Even when you have multiple birds in an aviary, the wings should be intact to help your bird escape an aggressive cage mate.

If you decide to clip your bird's wings, make sure you have it done at the vet's the first time. You can learn how to do it, practice with your vet and then do it at home. You need to be very experienced to ensure that you do not accidentally get any blood feathers.

A bird must be hand-tamed before you decide to clip his wings yourself. He must be comfortable enough to let you handle him. The first thing is to get your bird into a comfortable position to clip his wings. Pick him up using a towel and place him face down on your thigh. Then let the first wing out of the loose end of the towel and spread the feathers. Cut the primary feathers only. These are the largest feathers. The first three feathers are usually cut. You can snip about 1cm from each feather.

Then, repeat on the other side. Compare the wings to make sure that they are equal. If they are not, your bird will have difficulty walking or even perching. In case you do get a blood feather, make sure you apply styptic power to the wound immediately. If the bleeding does not stop, take the pet to the vet to have the shaft removed.

Clipping the wings only reduces your bird's ability to fly. It does not prevent flight altogether. So, when you take your bird outdoors, be vigilant. Even the slightest breeze can give him the lift he needs and lead to an escape. You need to clip the wings every 6 months.

3. Understanding cockatiel body language

Cockatiels use their crest for most of their communication. Learning about how the bird holds his crest or moves it can help you prevent a lot of accidents. It can also give you great insights to the bird's health.

Here are some signs that you can look out for:

- The crest is upright: The bird is surprised or scared. It can also mean that the bird is excited.

- The crest feathers are held flat against the head: This shows that the bird is angry. He will also bunch up his eyebrows to show aggression.

- The bird stands up tall and looks skinny: This means that he is startled. Most of the time, the crest is also upright when he does this.

- Head bobbing: If the bird has just been weaned, this is a sign of hunger. In older birds, it means that the bird wants your attention.

- The chest is puffed up: If he holds his wings back such that it makes a heart shaped formation, then the bird is bragging. It is usually a type of mating behavior.

- The head is lowered: The bird wants you to play or pet him.

- The body is lowered, he leans forward and the wings are half open: This is a sign that the bird is about to fly away but is unsure.

- The wings are spread out while the bird is on the topmost perch or on top of the cage: This is a sign that the bird is asserting his dominance over something.

- The bird pecks or bangs the beak on hard objects: This is very common in male cockatiels. This, too, is a sign of dominance.

- The bird paces and chirps: This means that he wants to come out of the cage. He may do this when he sees you and is eager to meet you.

- The bird nips your finger and then climbs onto it: While this may seem like the bird is trying to bite you, it only means that he is making sure that your finger is a safe perch.

- Beak grinding: This is a sign that the bird is content and happy.

- The bird sticks his body against yours or runs his beak on your body: This means that he wants to cuddle you.

- The head tilts up or turns sideways: He is looking at something from an odd position. This also means that he is curious about something.

- Tail rubbing: This is a sign that the cockatiel is masturbating.

- The head is held backwards with the eyes closed: This is a sign that the bird is getting ready to fall asleep.

- One eye is open and the other eye is closed while you are petting him: The bird is content but remains alert nevertheless.

- He yawns continuously: It is often a common preening behavior. It could also mean that the crop is being readjusted. He may even have something stuck in his throat.

- He rubs the head against his back: This is also preening behavior that is common to cockatiels.

- He is puffy and the body is lowered: The bird is about to poop. This is a very important body language sign when you are training your bird.

- The feathers are puffed up for a long time: This means that you need to take your bird to the vet.

- Rapid head shaking: This is a sign that the bird is experiencing a sudden change in temperature, humidity or even taste. Whenever he experiences a new sensation, the bird will shake his head quickly.

- He holds his wings out and becomes puffy when he is taking a bath: He is really enjoying himself.

- He seems to be sticking a toe in the nose and then making himself sneeze. This means that he is getting something out of his nose. If the behavior persists, you may want to take a look to make sure that the object has been removed.

- The ears and face get puffy: This is a sign that the bird is enjoying something that he hears.

- The wings are held up above his head: The bird is just stretching himself out.

4. Training your cockatiel

Even with timid birds like cockatiels, some basic training is required to make them easier to interact with. These birds are trainable to some extent and will respond to training if it is consistent and regular.

When you begin training a cockatiel, it is important to remember that they are not as human oriented as parrots. So, it may take much longer to train a cockatiel. If you have parrots or have friends who have any birds from the parrot family, you need to understand that your progress with your bird will be a lot slower.

Hand-raised birds are certainly easier to train. However, all birds can be trained if you get it right in the initial period. When you start training is the most crucial thing. It is best that you start when your bird is fully settled in the new cage.

It takes about a week for your cockatiels to get used to their new home. These birds are categorized as "high strung" when it comes to training, so you have to give them a lot of time to settle down.

Begin by getting the bird used to your hand. You need to place your hand in the bird's territory for some time. Offer treats like fruits or seeds when you do so. That way your bird will begin to associate your hand with positive reinforcement.

Repeat this until your bird is comfortable around your hand. There are chances that the bird will voluntarily alight on your finger if you try this consistently.

Finger training or step up training
It takes a lot of time to finger train cockatiels, but considering that these birds live up to 15 years of age or more, it is an important skill to teach your bird to make sure that you are able to get them away from situations that could be dangerous for them.

Try the above-mentioned process until the bird recognizes your hands as the source of the treat. The next step is to make sure that the bird comes to your hand and is willing to sit on your finger.

One trick that really helps is holding the treat just behind your finger and waiting for the bird to approach you. When the bird is comfortable enough, he will simply step up on your finger.

Continue this on a daily basis until your bird is sitting on your finger as soon as he sees it. The first step is to finger train your bird inside the cage before you actually let him out.

Getting the bird out of the cage
You need to study the body language of the bird. If he looks comfortable on your finger, you can take him out of the cage for a few minutes.

When you do this, you have to make sure that the area is safe for him. That means the doors and windows need to be shut, the fans need to be turned off and the pets in your household should be away from the area.

Take the cockatiel out and keep him on your finger for a few minutes outside the cage. In case he decides to fly away, it is a good idea to keep the cage door open and stay close to prevent the other birds from flying out.

After a few minutes, the bird will want to return to his companions. Having a bird that is hand-trained is easier to catch if he does not return on his own. That is why it is mandatory to carry out initial training inside the cage before you actually let him out. When he is back in the cage, give him a few treats to know that it is a positive space for him to go back to.

Teaching your cockatiel not to bite
There are two reasons why your cockatiel may bite: defense and attention. However, biting of any kind must be discouraged. The bird must know that it is not acceptable behavior. If you are able to build trust with the cockatiel, biting will significantly stop. There are other things that you can try to reduce stop your bird from biting.

In the initial days of your interaction with your cockatiel, biting only comes from fear, so you need to be patient. If your bird bites you when you are trying to get them to perch on your finger, you have to remember not to shout or scream.

The moment you do that, the bird gets a message that this is how they can control you and stop you from doing what they are not fond of. Instead, you just let the bird back in the cage and try again.

The next thing is when your cockatiel has started perching on your hand but begins to bite when you are trying to pet it. That is when you have a little more trust with the bird.

Then, you can gently push the head down with your index finger. It is a small and slight push that should not hurt the bird. Then in a very soft voice say "no biting". Then attempt to pet the cockatiel again until you have a positive reaction.

Just stroking the cheek is good. When this happens, praise the bird for being good, put the bird back in the cage and give him a closing treat. At this stage, the bird finds the cage to be a positive reinforcement.

The last type of biting that you want to discourage is "demand" bites. This is when you have established a good relationship with your bird and he nips at you when he wants something that is in your hand. For instance, if he is on your shoulder and you have a fruit in your hand, he will bit your ear or cheek. There are two things that you can do.

Firstly, you can just return the bird to the cage. This stops the behavior as the bird wants to be with you at this stage and going back to the cage is not as much fun as being with you.

The next thing is to shake his balance. If he is on your head or shoulder, you can actually run or jog. That puts the bird off balance and will make him release the beak. Now losing balance is something that cockatiels hate and they will give up any behavior that leads to it.

Stopping your cockatiel from screaming

As mentioned before, cockatiels can be extremely noisy. They can even begin to scream to seek attention or to make you do something they want you to. Both of these are not good and must be curbed.

Now, there are certain times of the day when the bird calls out instinctively. This is usually at dawn or dusk. Although this can be loud and extremely noisy, it is instinctive behavior. You must be sure that you can deal with some noise during the day. In addition, make sure your neighbors do not complain.

The only time the screaming becomes a problem is when your cockatiel begins to scream every time you leave the room. That means he is only screaming for your attention and nothing more. So, here are a couple of things that you do not want to do when you observe this behavior:

- Do not scream back at the bird and say, "Stop" or "Don't Scream".

- Do not come running back into the room every time to just get him to stop screaming. This encourages screaming. When you respond to with your own voice or by coming to the bird, you are doing exactly what they want. You are their "flock" that is calling back when they call, so they are happy to have your attention and will continue to scream.

- Unlike dogs or cats, a sharp "No!" is actually not a negative thing for birds. They think of it as your call in response to theirs.

- Instead, it is a good idea to put some toy or treat in the cage before you leave the room. That way they have something more interesting and something to distract them. It tells them that you going away means that it is time for some fun inside the cage.

- The next thing you can do is just let the bird scream and not come back. Wait for the screaming to stop and then go in and reward your bird. That way the bird understands that you will come back when he is quiet and will also reward him. Eventually, the period of silence will increase.

- Some people will tell you to put a blanket on the cage when the bird screams. While this works, it is negative reinforcement, hence it is discouraged.

Potty training

Surprisingly, it is possible for you to potty train a cockatiel. It just requires you to understand the pooping cycle and body language of your bird.

A small bird like a Green Cheek cockatiel will poop every 10 to 15 minutes and if you want to avoid accidents when your bird is out of the cage, you need to potty train him. Here are some simple tricks to teach your bird to poop where you want them to:

- The first thing to do would be to teach him to poop inside the cage in the morning.

- Before feeding, put a paper on the floor of the cage and wait for the bird to poop.

- They will show a very distinct type of body language, which is usually lifting their tail and leaning down on the perch. Then, when they do poop, praise them abundantly and offer a treat that is part of the diet.

- The next step is to watch for these signs after you have taught your bird to step up.

- When you see the pooping body language, hold them over a trash can or over a piece of paper. Then when they do poop on that, they need to be praised abundantly.

- That way, they know that there is one place or appropriate place for them to poop and they will not mess the whole house up.

Teaching cockatiels to talk

Unlike other species of parrots, cockatiels are not the best at learning to talk. They are intelligent enough to pick a few words and it is fun to teach them a few as well.

You need to choose what you want to teach them, as they can only pick up a few words. Cockatiels don't really learn the meaning of words but only learn to mimic you. They will associate it with a particular action, if you say the word before that action like a command. Here are a few tips to teach your cockatiel new words:

- Pick a word that you want to teach him. Suppose you pick, "hello", you need to say this everyday at a specific time.

- Make sure there are no distractions like TV sounds when you are saying the word that you want to teach him.

- Now associate that with an action that he will remember like you walking into a room.

- Say it in a high pitched sound and sound as excited as you can.

- If you are super excited, he will feel motivated to learn that call as it is positive to him.

- Eventually, when you enter the room, he will respond with a high pitched "hello". Be patient.

Chapter 6: Breeding your cockatiel

The good thing about breeding cockatiels is that they are extremely easy to pair up. However, for those who are looking at breeding commercially or really expect quality, you need to make sure that the birds that you breed are good natured, well-marked, well-shaped and large.

One of the most crucial things about breeding your cockatiel is ensuring that the bird is mature and has reached the breeding age. With cockatiels, the females reach sexual maturity at the age of 18 months. The males are sexually mature when they are about 12-15 months old.

Of course these birds can lay eggs when they are as young as six months old. However, when it comes to parenting, young birds are often known to abandon the nest. In addition to that, breeding too early can lead to health issues in birds as well.

1. Pairing up cockatiels

The first step is to determine whether you have a true pair. Do not take the word of the breeder or the pet store when it comes to the gender of the bird. With cockatiels, the best method to determine the gender is through DNA sexing. It is an inexpensive process that will help you create pairs faster.

When the birds are of the breeding age, they are most likely to accept a partner. However, if you are trying to introduce an older bird that has had a mate previously, it is a lot harder.

Never introduce the birds during the breeding season, as they tend to be more aggressive during this time. Do it a few months before. The first step is to place the bird in separate cages and place them side by side.

If there is no resistance, you can let both the birds out of the cage and allow them to interact in a neutral space under supervision. If the birds are calm and comfortable, you can place them in a cage together. Put them in a cage that is new to both of them to prevent any territorial behavior.

If you have to use an old cage, you must place the female inside before you introduce the male. You know that there is pair bonding between the birds if they sleep in the same nest box, sit on the perch together and preen each other. They may have spats once in a while. As long as it is not potentially dangerous, there is no need for you to interfere, as this behavior is quite normal for cockatiels.

When the birds are interested in a mate, they will exhibit certain mating behavior.

Female courting behavior
- She will sit very low with her tail in the air when she is on a perch.
- A typical peeping noise is made.
- She hangs upside down while keeping her the feathers of the tail spread out.
- She will rub the vent area on a toy or on the perch.
- She will try to feed the mate that she picks.

Male courting behavior
- He will tap his beak on any hard object such as the wire of the cage to get the attention of the female.
- He will have a strut accompanied by whistling, beak pounding, screaming and chattering.
- The top region of the wings are held away from the body. This makes a heart shape.
- He has a very typical whistle that is only reserved for courting.
- He will examine the nest box to make sure that it is safe for the female.

2. Getting the birds ready to breed

The cage needs to be prepared for Cockatiels to be able to breed properly. It is a good idea to give them a separate cage, which is enough to accommodate one pair. A smaller cage than the regular one can be used.

The good thing about cockatiels is that they do not require a fancy nesting box. Any size and shape is good enough for them as long as the pair can fit in comfortably. You can use an elongated cardboard box that measures about 10 inches in depth and height and about 24 inches in length. Using boxes that have an internal shelf can help you with your cockatiels. As these birds tend to push out most of the bedding when they are about to lay eggs, you will have to provide them with new bedding every time. With an internal shelf type nesting box, the bedding will collect in the bottom and you can just replace it as long as it is clean.

It is best that you provide your bird with lot of natural light. If that is not possible, then you can use a fluorescent light. Full spectrum lights can be placed near the cage to give the bird about 13 hours of daylight. If the light is provided for longer, the birds will breed all year long.

Position the breeding cage against the wall in a quiet area. This will give your bird a sense of security. When they are against the wall, they know that they will not have any threat from that side.

Feeding the breeding birds
Your birds will need a lot of good food to lay healthy and fertile eggs. A balanced meal that contains about 35% fresh produce, 20% seed and 45% formulated pellets is the best option.

Try to give your cockatiel more fruits in comparison to vegetables in this season. As they prefer sweet foods, they will consume it more readily.

One of the most important nutrients for cockatiels in this season is amino acids. They are available from foods like meat, which is not really the natural diet for the bird. That is why you need to give them a vet-recommended formulated pellet diet. A piece of yellow cheese or eggs can also help your bird, and additional protein is required when the bird is entering the breeding season. Your vet may recommend larvae that is available in pet stores.

Calcium is another essential nutrient to ensure that the eggs are synthesized properly. You will notice that females will begin to compulsively chew on objects that provide a source of minerals. Giving your bird cuttlebone is a good idea. The mineral blocks that are available in pet stores are usually rejected by cockatiels. If the bird does not get enough calcium, she will chew on plaster on the walls and even on brick surfaces.

If the bird is ignoring cuttlebones as well, you can give them an oyster shell. Calcium supplements can also be recommended by the vet.

3. Artificial Incubation
It is best that you allow the parents to hatch the eggs and then take over the responsibility of feeding the birds by hand in order to make them acquainted with people.

Artificial incubation is not always necessary. There are a few breeding problems that arise, making it necessary for you to hatch the eggs in an incubator.

Egg breaking or eating
This is a common issue with birds that have been brought into captivity from the wild. This is only a result of the bird's defensive behavior towards anyone who approaches the nest.

The bird sits or jumps on the egg as an attempt to safeguard it and ends up breaking the eggs. This is when you have to take the following precautions:

- Increase the size of the cage or enclosure.
- Make the nesting box narrower and darker.
- Minimize any activity in the breeding area of the birds and make it as quiet as possible.

In some cases, this habit is repeated with every clutch and is actually just a learnt behavior pattern. This is when you will have to intervene and incubate the eggs artificially.

Abandonment of the eggs
Smaller birds like cockatiels are notorious for abandoning their eggs. You will face this problem more often with hand-raised parent birds that do not have any parenting instinct. This is when you can take one of the following measures:

- Pair a hand raised bird with one raised by the natural parents. That way one is experienced and the other can learn.

- If your hen is not a good breeder, you need to take the decision of taking the bird out of the breeding program. While this may be hard for you to do, you need to understand that these birds are just not meant to care for a clutch.

- If your birds have been good parents in the past, then you need to check the nesting conditions that you have provided. If anything seems out of the ordinary or inappropriate, making the necessary changes will prevent abandonment.

If you notice any of the above problems with the clutch, you will have to incubate the eggs artificially. Collect the eggs carefully and place them in a commercially available incubator. You will have the details of all the settings for cockatiel eggs. Once you have set the incubator as needed, you have to follow these measures to make sure that you get maximum hatchability with your eggs:

- Place the incubator in an area that is free from any direct sunlight or drafts.

- The incubator should be sterilized before you place the eggs inside.

- The web bulb wick and the humidifier must be functioning properly.

- Make sure you wash your hands and clean the eggs thoroughly before you put them in the incubator. They should be free from any dirt or grime.

- The small end or the pointed end of the egg should always be lower than the large end of the egg.

- The egg must be turned at least 5 times a day. If you fail to turn the eggs every day, chances are that the chicks that are developing will get stuck to one side and may be born with the organ sticking out of the body.

- Once you have set the eggs inside the incubator do not disturb them, except for when you turn them. While doing so, if you notice that the eggs are still cold, chances are that you have not started the incubator or that it is not functioning properly.

- It is possible to check the progress of your eggs with a bucket of water. In the beginning the eggs will sink to the bottom while towards the end of the incubation period, they will begin to float on the surface.

Once the eggs have hatched, you need to shift the chicks to a brooder. You may choose to place the bird in a commercially available brooder or may make one using a box and the appropriate full spectrum light. The temperature should be around 92 degree F when the birds just hatch. By the 5th day you can reduce this to 80 degree F.

You will have to place absorbent bedding such as newspaper. Keeping the brooder moisture level above 50% is very important. If you are making a brooder at home, you can use a spray bottle to mist the brooder with lukewarm, distilled water. Make sure you only spray around the brooder and never directly at the chick.

4. Hand feeding your cockatiels

- You can get the feeding formula from any local pet store. Make a mixture of this formula with hot water and place it in a sterilized container. The formula should be made freshly before every feeding session and should never be stored in the refrigerator.

- Force-feeding chicks is strictly prohibited. If you hold up a teaspoon or a syringe to the bird, he should approach you voluntarily. This reduces chances of choking on the food.

- As the chick feeds he will bob his head up and down. You will have to match the rhythm of dispensing food with this rhythm.

- Pause and give the food in short intervals to help the bird swallow better.

- The formula must never fall on the nostrils of the bird. If you notice any on the beak or nostril, clean it immediately.

- Never overfeed the chick. If he stops eating, do not force him.

- The crop should empty before you give the bird his feed.

Increase the consistency of the formula with each day. By day 5 you can start weaning the chicks. Leave the food around and see if they eat on their own. By the 8th day, you can stop feeding the bird at night. That will make them hungry enough to eat by themselves. By the time they are 21 days old, they should be fully weaned.

Hand feeding is a great option if you wish to sell the chicks. Most people prefer birds that are already used to human interaction in order to make it easier during the housebreaking phase. These birds are also much easier to train.

In some cases where the parents are caring for their young, you can try mixed feeding. Allow the parent birds to give the chicks one meal and you can give them the next until they are weaned. These are the most sought after types of birds, as they have the experience of being parented and are also comfortable around human beings

5. Development issues

There are a few developmental issues that you may notice in the hatchlings within the first few days. The most common issues are:

- Straddled leg or spayed legs: To prevent this, you can keep the young birds in a small bowl so that the legs stay right under their body. They must not be placed on smooth surfaces that do not provide them with enough grip. Feed the birds when they are standing on some surface like paper to give them good support. If the condition is very severe you will have to use surgical tape to hold the legs closer to each other.

- Misdirected toe: This is a toe that will not point in the direction that is normal. For parrots it is common to have two toes pointing forward and two back. However, in some cases, they may be born with three toes pointing forward. In the first few days, the toe will turn backwards on its own. If this does not happen properly, then you will have to tape the toe to the one that is facing in the right direction for about a week. Eventually, it will stay in the right position.

- Constricted toe: This is when the skin on the toe becomes very tight and prevents blood flow. This requires a trip to the vet to have it surgically corrected.

Development issues are often the result of improper nutrition, so you need to make sure that you do not compromise on your bird's diet.

Chapter 7: Proper Cockatiel Healthcare

Like any other bird, the health of the cockatiel is also sensitive. Although these birds are hardier than most other species of parrots, it is very important to make sure that you take good care of its health. This includes proper nutrition, good sanitation and adequate exercise as well.

In this chapter we discuss all the aspects of your bird's health from finding an avian vet who is qualified, to looking for the possible insurance plans for your bird.

1. Finding an avian vet

A regular vet is not what you need for your cockatiel. Birds are extremely different from other pets. The anatomy and the basic requirement of these creatures are very different, so you need to have a certified avian vet who can help your bird.

Avian vets have a degree in veterinary medicine but have dedicated a large portion of their practice to birds. Every country has an association that vets can register under to stay updated about this science. One such association is the Association of Avian Vets or AAV. You can find all the registered avian vets in your vicinity using their official website which is www.aav.org.

If you are unable to find a good avian vet on this website, you have the option of asking a regular vet for leads. You may also contact cockatiel clubs in your city for more information.

When you are choosing an avian vet, here are a few things that you need to look for:

- Staff that is trained to handle birds. They will be comfortable around your birds and will know a little bit about the species as well.

- There should be an emergency facility linked with the clinic in case your bird needs immediate attention. It is best to look for a clinic that even has a pet hospital for in-house patients.

- The vet should have mostly avian patients. If he/she is only seeing one or two birds in a day, he/she is most likely not an avian vet. Some of the avian vets also deal with exotic pets like reptiles but will dedicate most of their practice to birds.

- Each examination should be for at least 30 minutes. If the interval between each patient is just about 15 minutes, your bird may not be getting a thorough examination.

- The clinic should be as close to your home as possible. Drives are extremely stressful for pets and should be minimal.

Your avian vet should also be updated with the facilities available for birds. If he is part of the AAV or attends regular seminars about avian medicine, you can be sure that your bird is in great hands.

2. Checking for signs of illnesses

There are several symptoms that help you identify a sick bird. These symptoms can either be mild or intense. In any case, you have to be alert and identify the slightest change or deviation from normal. That can work wonders in saving your bird's life.

Here are a few symptoms that can help you identify illnesses in your birds and provide timely assistance:

- **Fluffed feathers**
  If your bird looks fluffy or puffed up in appearance, it is the most obvious sign of an ill bird. The common reason for fluffing up feathers is to keep himself warm.

  When your bird tries to do this, you will see that the regular sleek frame is lost. The bird will actually look fat and extremely messy. Sometimes birds may just puff up their feathers for some time while preening, but if the puffiness is prolonged, it is a matter of great concern.

  However, puffiness must never be ignored even if the bird retracts the feathers when you approach him. This is a common defense mechanism, as the bird does not look vulnerable. You must also be observant of the bird's body language. If the bird looks sick or you have the slightest suspicion, you need to make sure that you pay attention.

- **Wet vent**
If the vent area of the bird is constantly wet, then it can be considered a symptom of illness. This is the underside of the bird where the bird excretes from. If the bird is healthy, the vent is dry and clean.

- **Respiratory issues**
One of the most common telltale signs of sickness in a bird is abnormal or heavy breathing. This type of breathing without any physical exertion means that the bird may be unwell. In addition to heavy breathing, the bird will also exhibit tail bobbing.

If the bird is sneezing, coughing or has some sort of nasal discharge, it is an indication of illness. Hold the bird close to you if you have any suspicion. You may be able to hear a distinct clicking sound, which indicates chances of mites or parasites in the air sac. This needs to be checked immediately to help the bird recover at the earliest.

- **Inactivity**
Cockatiels are usually quite active and love to fly about or just interact with one another. If your bird is sleepy all the time and is found catching untimely naps, it is a warning sign.

Birds will nap in the afternoons or during the day. However, they seldom nap when the rest of their cage mates are active. If your bird is snoozing while the others are active, you need to look at it as a warning sign.

Birds that sit at the bottom of the cage for long hours may also be unwell. If they have the habit of sitting on the floor of the cage, it will usually be with their partners.

However, if you see that your cockatiels are shunning the company of other birds, especially their own partners, you need to understand that there is definitely some problem with the bird.

- **Loss of appetite**
  If a bird loses interest in food because of any illness, it is a sign of great concern. Always be observant of your birds. The thing with cockatiels is that they do not want to appear unwell or sick. They may just pretend to eat the food you have given to them to make sure that they do not look vulnerable. However, they could only be sifting through the food and may not be actually consuming anything.

- **Lack of singing**
  Vocalization is the most important sign of health. These birds are known for their unique songs and vocalization patterns.

  When birds are unwell they remain unusually silent. The idea behind this is to make sure that they do not attract any unwanted attention from predators.

  In addition to this, birds that are unwell will also do this as a method of saving up their energy. If a bird who normally loves to chirp and sing becomes abnormally silent, you must immediately take him to your vet.

- **Unusual droppings**
  Whenever you are cleaning out the substrate of the cage, make sure that you check the droppings of the birds. If the droppings are abnormal or have some unusual color, it could be a sign of indigestion or some disease.

  If you have several birds in your aviary that belong to different families and species, this can be a little challenging. However, you can watch out for a few basic things such as the urates, which should be white and dry in color. On the other hand, if it dries up to look green or yellow, you need to show some concern immediately.

  The maintenance of cockatiels depends mostly on simple observation. If you are unable to spend time watching your birds, you will never become familiar with the regular and normal behavior. As a result, you will also be unable to identify anything out of the ordinary.

In fact, you may miss out on initial symptoms of diseases that can be managed fairly easily. Even if you stop paying attention for a short time, you can miss out on some important behavioral changes that can be pivotal in saving the bird's life.

One thing all bird owners should know about is that birds prefer to hide their illness in order to look fit. In most cases, by the time the symptom becomes obvious, the bird is already very sick.

If you have an aviary, a sick bird is not only a matter of concern because of his health. He is a ticking time bomb that can affect the rest of the flock in no time.

If you are observant and find the symptoms early, you can have the bird quarantined and ensure that the rest of your flock is safe too. You have to first identify that your bird is sick. The next step is to narrow in on which disease it actually is. Lastly, you need to take all the preventive measures necessary for your aviary in order to keep the birds healthy.

3. Common health issues in cockatiels

There are a few health issues that you will find common to most types of parrots. Unfortunately, most of these conditions manifest late and put the bird at the risk of permanent damage and in severe cases, death. Make sure that you learn in as much detail as possible about these conditions to prevent them and also to identify the possibility of your bird developing the condition.

This section lists all the causes, symptoms, diagnosis methods and the outcome of the condition or the prognosis of each condition that is likely to affect cockatiels.

Aspergillosis

Transmission

- The condition is transmitted by a type of mold called *Aspergillus fumigatus*.
- It is a condition that humans may contract as well.
- It is usually transmitted from the parent to the chick.

- If the concentration of mold is too high in the air, the water or the food, the birds may be infected.
- It is also transmitted in cages that are over-crowded.

Symptoms

- Labored breathing
- Inability to vocalize or rasping when the bird tries to vocalize
- Anorexia
- Depression
- Loss of control on bodily movements
- Nasal discharge
- Lesions in the eyes
- Inflammation of the eyes .

Diagnosis

- Polymerase chain reaction test
- Anti-body titer

Prognosis
- The condition leads to complications in the respiratory system.
- The mold may colonize in several organs of the body leading to organ or tissue damage.
- Nebulization is an option to control the condition.
- It may lead to death in most cases as the infection can be severe.

Avian flu or influenza

Transmission

- The condition is transmitted from the infected bird through water, food, nasal or oral discharge.
- Hardy viruses may be present when the temperature is not properly controlled. The lower the temperature, the higher the chances of contracting this condition.

- Although there are few recorded cases, this condition may affect human beings as well.

Symptoms

- Depression
- Lethargy
- Loss of limb control
- Loss of appetite
- Inability to stand or walk
- Staying close to the floor of the cage
- Labored breathing
- The bird is unable to stay stable on a perch.

Diagnosis

- Usually this condition leads to death in the birds and the diagnosis only occurs when the body of the bird is examined through a necropsy.

Prognosis
- There is very little you can do if the bird is diagnosed with this condition. It is 100% fatal in most cases.

Avian tuberculosis

Transmission

- It is caused by a type of bacteria called *mycobacterium avium*.
- It is generally transmitted through the feces.
- It can also be transmitted from contaminated food or water.
- Some birds may be carriers of the condition and an increased concentration of the pathogen in the environment leads to infections.

Symptoms

- The birds develop a lumpy mass under the skin
- Chronic wasting

- Diarrhea
- Swollen joints
- Lameness
- Depression.

Diagnosis

- Microscopic examination of the lab cultures
- Biopsy
- Endoscopy.

Prognosis

- The condition is very common in birds that are housed outdoors or when they are imported.
- Strict isolation or quarantining is one of the best ways to treat the condition.

Chlamydiosis or parrot fever

Transmission

- The condition is transmitted by a microorganism called *Chlamydiophila psittaci.*
- It is transmitted through any discharge from the eye or the nasal area.
- This organism is very hardy and has the ability to survive in any dried feces.
- This microorganism is a threat to human beings and can cause severe infections.

Symptoms

- Labored breathing
- Loss of appetite
- Depression
- Lethargy
- Diarrhea

- Sudden weight loss
- Yellow or green droppings
- Nasal discharge
- Discharge from the eyes.

Diagnosis

- PCR tests
- Blood tests
- Cloacal swab test
- Observation of a laboratory culture of the microorganism.

Prognosis

- Usually the bird will recover from the condition when it is detected early.
- A six week cycle of doxycycline is recommended.
- Preventive measures are a must, as repeated infection will lead to respiratory problems that can be permanent.

Glardiasis

Transmission

- The microorganism responsible for this condition is present in the feces.
- It can also be transmitted through food or water that is contaminated.
- Glardiasis can be transmitted from the bird to humans.

Symptoms

- Feather plucking
- Sudden weight loss
- Bright yellow or green colored urates
- Nutritional deficiency
- Diarrhea

Diagnosis

- There are several tests that are available but this condition is not detected reliably.
- In most cases, the response to the treatment is the only way to diagnose the condition.

Prognosis

- Treatment can be prolonged if the bird is still showing symptoms and of there is a chance of a bird being a carrier.
- The entire flock must be treated to prevent repeated infection.
- Medication like metronidazole and rhonidazole are recommended for effective management of the condition.
- Immune support is provided in the form of a good diet and exercise.

Newcastle's Disease

Transmission

- This condition is normally transmitted through the feces.
- Other sources of infection include nasal discharge, ocular discharge, contaminated food or water.
- The pathogen is quite hardy and can be present in the environment for several days in the right conditions.
- This is another disease that may affect human beings as well.

Symptoms

- Usually there are no signs in the initial stages. The symptoms occur only after the bird is severely infected.
- Depression
- Paralysis
- Dyspnea
- Loss of appetite
- Weight loss
- Impairment of neurological function.

Diagnosis

- In most cases the condition is diagnosed only when the body of a bird is inspected after death.

Prognosis

- For most parrot species the chances of recovery are poor.
- Even when the bird does recover, he could be a carrier of the condition.
- Usually, the bird dies before the condition can be managed.

Psittacine beak and feather disease

Transmission

- Infection is caused by *Psittacine Circovirus* 1 or *Psittacine Circovirus* 2.
- It is usually transmitted through feather dander, blood or feces.
- The condition can be transmitted when the parent feeds the chick.
- It can also be transferred from the parent to the egg.
- This is a hardy virus that can survive in the environment from about 6 months to 2 years.

Symptoms

- Sudden feather loss
- Deformity in the feather
- Depression in the chicks
- Vomiting
- Lesions in the feathers
- Deformity or sudden degradation of the beak.

Diagnosis

- Blood tests
- Feather biopsy

- Examination of the body post death.

Prognosis

- In most cases the adults will be immune to the condition after being affected once. However, they may shed the virus or be carriers.
- Supportive care is the only option as there is no recommended treatment available.
- It usually results in the death of the infected bird, especially if they are young.

Polyomavirus

Transmission

- The virus can be transmitted through the feces, feather dander or by inhalation of the virus present in the environment.
- It can be passed on from the hen to the chick.
- The virus is potent and can survive in the environment for several years.
- There are vaccinations available for newly hatched chicks.
- Chicks are most likely to be affected by the condition.

Symptoms

- Weight loss
- Delayed emptying of the crop
- Anorexia
- Depression
- Vomiting
- Bleeding in the subcutaneous region
- Diarrhea.

Diagnosis

- Blood tests
- Cloacal swab tests

- Necropsy or examination after the death of the bird.

Prognosis

- If the chicks are infected, they will die within 48 hours.
- Adults may recover from the condition but will remain carriers most often.
- There is no specific treatment available.
- Supportive care is the best option to manage this condition.

Avian bornavirus

Transmission
- This is an enveloped virus that is less likely to survive outside the host.
- It is transmitted when birds come into contact with contaminated bodily fluids, food or feces.
- The carriers will normally not show any symptoms of the condition.
- This is one of the least known diseases with no exact details on the incubation, prevalence and etiology.

Symptoms

- Weight loss
- Impaired flight and balance
- Anorexia
- Depression
- Vomiting
- Wing flipping
- Abnormality in the movement of the head
- Toe tapping
- Motor deficit.

Diagnosis

- Usually necropsy is the only option
- You will notice ganglia in the autonomic and peripheral nerves.
- Crop biopsy will reveal lesions.

Prognosis

- The bird will usually die in about 11 days of being infected or may survive for about 7 years with supportive care.
- There is no method of reliable treatment. Some medicines for the virus and the inflammation have been used experimentally.
- Good nutrition and quarantining measures will help you assist the bird in the recovery process.

Pacheco's disease

Transmission

- This is a type of herpesvirus that is transmitted through nasal and ocular discharge.
- The virus does not survive for long in the environment.
- Birds that are carriers will shed the virus that can only survive with a host.

Symptoms

- Anorexia
- Diarrhea
- Sinusitis
- Diarrhea with blood
- Tremors
- Head tilting
- Seizures
- Excessive thirst
- Excessive urination
- Green or yellow droppings.

Diagnosis

- Blood test
- Cloacal swab test
- Necropsy or examination after death.

Prognosis

- Most birds will recover fully.
- Supportive care is the best option.
- There are a few recommended anti viral medicines that may be administered to the bird.

Psittacine papillomatosis

Transmission

- This is also a type of herpes virus.
- Close contact with infected birds through feeding or when preening can lead to infection.

Symptoms

- Lesions in the oral cavity
- Whitish, scaly warts in the mouth
- Lesions on the feet and toes
- Lesions in the cloaca
- Lesions on the eye or the eyelid
- Anorexia
- Vomiting
- Infertility
- Prolapse in the cloaca.

Diagnosis

- A tissue that is affected by pappilomatus will turn white when 5% acetic acid is added to it.
- Endoscopy
- Examination of lesions
- Necropsy.

Prognosis

- The lesions must be removed surgically or with a laser.
- If the GI tract is severely infected, it will lead to the bird's death.

You can consult your vet to stay updated with any developments in the treatment of the serious conditions. The more you learn, the more likely you are to spot the condition and look for timely assistance to help your bird.

4. Nutrition-related issues

Birds are quicker than any other creature in the animal kingdom to depict the signs of malnutrition.

In most cases, the immunity of the bird towards disease-causing organisms is compromised when his nutritional requirements are not met.

It is very common to see birds showcase nutritional problems when they are in the breeding cycle. Problems like calcium deficiency are most prevalent in these birds. This leads to a lot of complications like egg binding or prolapse of the oviduct.

Each species has a different type of response to deficits in nutrition. In the case of the cockatiels, you will see a lot of telltale signs. The most common nutritional diseases in cockatiels include:

Obesity

This is the most common nutritional disorder, often ending in hepatic lipidosis or fatty liver. This condition has been observed in birds that are usually on a high fat, seed only diet. This type of diet also leads to other issues like lowered calcium in the blood. Seeds also lack nutrients like vitamin A.

Two organs of the bird's body that are normally affected by obesity are the liver and the heart. Over time, all the fat that has accumulated in the blood is passed on into the liver. This leads to a drastic decrease in the amount of functional tissue in the liver.

This condition also makes the liver very enlarged. If the fat accumulation occurs around the heart of the bird, the normal functioning of the heart is also compromised.

If the bird is overweight, he is not able to perform simple tasks such as flying or bathing in the water trough.

Symptoms of hepatic lipidosis

- Fat deposits are seen on the abdomen and chest, making these areas look large and buxom.

- The beak tends to grow rather abnormally. This condition is often identified by those who groom the bird and trim the beak at the vet's office.

- You will see obvious black spots on the toenails and the beak. This is primarily because the functionality of the liver is compromised. The clotting of blood does not occur properly, leading to bruise-like splotches on the beak and the nails.

- The liver is enlarged. Of course, this is not seen visually. When the bird is being checked by the vet, this becomes obvious. In smaller birds like cockatiels, you can see this enlarged liver through the screen if you just moisten the skin with some alcohol.

These clinical signs are noticed in birds of all species. If you do not curb the fat intake of your bird, the regular bodily functions are largely compromised. Even simple stress like a loud noise can be too stressful for the bird leading to death.

Diagnosis

- Physical examinations are the first step to diagnosis.

- Your vet may also require the blood to be tested for anemia, lipemia or chances of jaundiced plasma which indicate compromised functioning of the liver.

Treatment

The best way to manage this condition is by improving the nutrition of your bird. You can prevent this condition entirely if you are careful about what you are feeding the bird.

Make sure that your bird gets a good balance of homemade food as well as commercially available food for the best possible results.

Some medicines such as probenecid or colchicine can be administered to help birds that have been severely affected.

Hypovitaminosis A

This is yet another condition that you will see in birds that have been maintained on an all seed diet. Most seeds and nuts do not have any traces of vitamin A.

The mucous membrane and the epithelial tissue is maintained by Vitamin A. When the levels of this nutrient drop, resistance to pathogenic or disease-causing organisms also decreases.

You will commonly notice infections of the sinus and the respiratory tract in birds that have a deficiency of Vitamin A. You will also notice scaliness, flakiness and thickening of the skin of the bird's feet.

Symptoms of Vitamin A deficiency

- White plaques are seen on the roof of the mouth.

- A change in the functionality of the tear glands and the salivary glands leads to high levels of oral mucous.

- Respiratory difficulty accompanied by problems like coughing are quite common in birds with this condition.

- When the lack of vitamin A leads to compromised immunity, it manifests in the form of abscesses in the respiratory tract, the crop and the oral cavity of the bird.

- In case of brightly colored birds such as cockatiels, the coloration of the plumage will also fade away with time.

- The hatchability rate of the clutches will decrease quite drastically.

- The chicks that do hatch may not survive or may fail to gain weight and die eventually.

Treatment

Preventive measures such as a healthy diet and proper supplementation are the best options for your bird. In case your bird develops this condition despite all the care, here are a few things that you can try:

- Provide commercial feed that is fortified with Vitamin A. These foods are often given along with water.

- The amount of orange and red vegetables as well as green leafy vegetables should be increased in your bird's diet.

- You can provide your bird with beta-carotene supplements. In most clinical cases, this supplement is injected.

- Add a few drops of the extracts from a Vitamin A gel capsule into your bird's food.

- Cod liver oil can be added to your bird's diet. This is also quite easy to mix with dry foods like pellets and seeds.

With a balanced vitamin A intake, you will notice that your birds become more and more resistant to common health issues. You will also notice a very positive change in the reproductive cycle and results with regular Vitamin A supplements.

Hypervitaminosis A

Just as the deficiency of nutrients can lead to a lot of health problems, an excess of the same nutrient can be toxic to the bird. Many bird owners tend to over-supplement the diet of their birds, leading to several complications.

The only sad thing is that this is a poorly documented condition among birds. In other animals, it has been seen that an excess of vitamin A in the body leads to a lot of fatigue and weakness in the bird. It can also lead to pain in the bones.

Calcium, Vitamin D3 and Phosphorous imbalance

If the diet of your bird consists mainly of oily seeds and grains, you will notice these imbalances. These foods have a very low ratio of phosphorous to calcium and are also deficient in Vitamin D3. Additionally, the calcium that is available to the bird is bound within the body in the form of soaps when the diet is too oily.

Calcium is one of the most important minerals as far as birds are concerned. The production of the egg is highly hampered when the calcium intake is not high enough. Calcium is also required by the skeleton of the bird. If calcium and phosphorous are not absorbed properly, it can lead to bones that are underdeveloped or extremely fragile.

There are several other bodily functions such as the transmission of nerve impulses, muscle contractions and also metabolic processes that are affected by the calcium levels in the body.

Calcium metabolism is affected by the amount of Vitamin D3 and phosphorous in the bird's body. Therefore, providing only calcium is meaningless, as it will not be utilized properly.

Ideally, the ration of calcium to phosphorous should be 2:1 in the body of birds like cockatiels. This value can have a 0.5 variation and not more.

Symptoms of calcium, vitamin D3 and phosphorous imbalance

- Adult birds are highly uncoordinated in muscle function when there is an imbalance.
- Weakness is commonly seen in birds with this nutritional deficiency.
- Egg binding as well as paresis or fatigue is seen in egg laying birds that do not have enough calcium available in their diet.
- In the case of chicks you will see that deformities in the bones and joints are very common.
- Spay leg formation is seen in birds that have a lower calcium intake.

Treatment

Supplementation is the best option when your bird has calcium deficiency. However, you need to be very careful when you are giving these supplements to your birds.

If not done properly, excessive amounts of phosphorous and calcium can lead to other complications.

If the level of calcium is beyond the necessary amount, it can lead to mineralization of the kidney and kidney failure. When calcium is available in large amounts, the absorption of essential trace elements like zinc and manganese is affected.

If the level of phosphorous is too high, it is seen that calcium is not absorbed properly. This is because any calcium in the body will be bound in the form of calcium phosphate that is not soluble. As a result, the blood calcium level will be low.

You need to make sure that you do not provide any unwanted supplements if the natural foods are able to provide your bird with all the nutrients that he requires.

Imbalance in Vitamin D
The main function of Vitamin D is to make sure that calcium metabolism occurs in the body of the bird. Vitamin D can be equally problematic if the levels are either too low or too high.

If the diet of the bird consists of an excessive amount of Vitamin D, it leads to toxicosis, which means that the amount of calcium absorbed by the body also increases drastically. In the initial stages this is not an issue, as the kidney is able to excrete the excess calcium out, but with repetitive calcium excess, the function of the kidney is compromised leading to a reduced rate of glomerular filtration. As a result kidney stones are formed and can be extremely painful for your birds.

There are several factors such as the form of Vitamin D ingested, the amount of calcium and vitamin A in the diet etc. that determine the chances of toxicosis. The health of the kidney is another major factor.

For example, providing cholecalciferol vitamin D supplements are more toxic than supplements like ergocalciferol. In fact, the former puts the bird at 10 times more risk than the latter.

If your bird is being over-supplemented with vitamin D, there are chances that the kidney gets mineralized along with calcification of the blood. If you have fed your bird toxic amounts of Vitamin D3, you may balance it out by reducing calcium in the diet.

If your bird has any nutritional imbalance, the best thing to do would be to provide the bird with a diet that is nutritionally adequate. Getting them on homemade food is the best option. Of course, you also have the option of providing them with recommended commercial foods.

Mineral sources like calcium carbonate that can be found in egg or oyster shells are ideal for cockatiels. You can also give your bird natural sources like milk, yoghurt, cheese, spinach and broccoli. If you are giving your bird eggs, make sure that it is not raw to reduce any risk of salmonellosis.

Iodine deficiency
A seed-based diet is usually responsible for iodine deficiency in the body. Thyroxine, which is responsible for thyroid gland function, is not formed in the body without adequate amounts of iodine.

It is necessary to give your bird iodine supplements if you are keeping them on a seed only diet. This supplement can be added into the food or water of the bird

Goiter is the result of iodine deficiency. The thyroid gland is present in the area where the trachea branches out into the lungs. This is just above the heart. As a result, when these glands become enlarged, a lot of pressure is applied on the voice box and the trachea. You will notice that birds have great difficulty breathing when they suffer from iodine deficiency for this very reason.

You will notice a wheeze, click or a squeaking sound whenever your bird tries to breathe. You will also notice vomiting in birds that have an iodine deficiency.

Goiter develops very slowly but gets very bad progressively. The larger the thyroid gets, the more obvious the sounds while breathing become. In many cases, the bird needs to exert himself physically and hold his head up in order to breathe.

There is always a chance of secondary bacterial invasion or fungal infection. This condition also leads to weight gain, deposits of fat on the internal organs, compromised feather quality and a lot of other secondary issues.

Although this is a rare deficiency in cockatiels, you need to be watchful. The treatment of the condition is determined by the severity of deficiency.

Treatment of iodine deficiency

- In the case of a mild deficiency, adding iodine supplements in the food or water can help.

- In extreme cases, your bird may have to be hospitalized to receive sodium iodide injections daily until this condition is reversed.

- Preventive measures are important following the treatment in the form of good diet and necessary supplements.

Hemochromatosis
Iron storage disease or hemochromatosis is very common and is the result of the bird's inability to excrete any excessive iron. This leads to damage in the heart, kidneys and the liver. Blood breakdown and chronic stress can be caused by hemochromatosis.

Several enzymes are not formed when there is an excess of iron in the body. In addition to that, it also leads to a genetic predisposition of the hatchlings to this condition.

You will notice difficulty in breathing along with a distension of the abdomen. Discolored droppings are common with birds who have hemochromatosis.

Treatment of hemochromatosis

- Long-term phlebotomies or bloodletting is carried out on a weekly basis in order to reduce the iron deposits.

- The iron levels in blood serum are constantly monitored to ensure that they do not exceed 150mg.

- A hematocrit or CBC is used to make sure that the bird recovers from these blood-letting sessions.

- A medicine called deferozamine has been used to treat this condition as well.

Dietary management is the best way to prevent this condition in your cockatiels. All you need to do is consult your vet. Bottled water is recommended if your bird has had this condition in the past.

Birds that have not had hemochromatosis and have lived long lives have been given a lot of fresh food and low amounts of seeds. It is best that you also rely on a balanced diet for your birds to prevent the above-mentioned nutritional deficiency.

If you are new to the world of cockatiels it is recommended that you follow a diet provided by your vet to the T. As you gain more experience with your birds and do your own research, you can mix up the diet. In any case, remember that supplementation without consultation is always prohibited for your birds if you want to ensure that they stay in the best of their health for the rest of their lives.

5.First aid for cockatiels

Birds can have several injuries on a day-to-day basis and will need immediate and correct assistance. Make sure that you always have the emergency contact numbers handy and also a well-maintained first aid kit to help your bird in time when it is needed.

The common injuries are:

- Broken wings or blood feathers: This may occur when you are trying to clip the feathers or due to the feathers getting stuck in toys, etc. If the wing is broken, hold it close to the body and secure it with non-sticky tape or gauze. Make sure you don't tape it too tightly, as it will cause breathing issues.

If a blood feather breaks you will see lot of blood loss. You can just dab some styptic powder or flour on the area. Then, hold it down with some gauze and apply pressure to stop bleeding.

- Attack by a cat, dog or other bird: The first thing that you need to do is calm the bird down. You can place him in a separate cage in a quiet room. Then, examine the injuries. Bleeding can be stopped with styptic powder, flour and gauze. Treat a broken feather as mentioned above. The bird must be taken to a vet immediately, as the saliva of a cat or dog can be toxic to birds.

- Abrasions and wounds: In the event that a bird comes into contact with a sharp surface, wounds may be caused. The first step is to clean the wound with hydrogen peroxide, then take out any dirt or sharp objects using tweezers. You must also remove any feathers that are stuck on the wound. An antibiotic cream will help the wound heal. Make sure that your bird does not pick at the wound, as it will become deeper.

- Breathing issues: If you see strained breathing in your bird, check the nostrils for any foreign objects. Carefully remove the object using a pair of tweezers. Breathing with the mouth open indicates exhaustion or overheating. Outstretched wings mean that the bird needs to be cooled down instantly. That can be done by placing the bird in a dish of cold water or by holding a wet towel around his body. If you do not see blockage or heating, then the breathing issue is the result of an underlying illness that needs to be examined by a vet immediately.

- Burns: The area that is affected should be washed under running water immediately. You can then dab the area with gauze to dry it up. For mild burns, an ice pack will provide significant relief. If it is a major burn, rush the bird to a vet. You must also take care to calm the bird down, as a burn can lead to a lot of trauma.

- Chilling: If the bird is exposed to air conditioning or heavy drafts, it may lead to chilling. The body can be warmed up using a warm towel or a heat lamp. The temperature must be raised gradually. Overheating after chilling is quite common if the bird is in shock or if he has been injured. Thoroughly check the bird's environment for any chances of drafts. The best option is to relocate your bird's cage if you notice any issues.

- Toxication: The bird may come into physical contact with toxins or may inhale them. The most common sources of toxins are sprays, paint or even an AC vent. If the bird has ingested a toxin, it is a major cause for concern and you must call your vet immediately. You can even call any poison control authority in your area for immediate assistance. In this case, you will have to provide them with all details including the symptoms, the toxin the bird may have consumed and the amount of toxin consumed.

With timely assistance, most of these issues can be dealt with. The more you are observant of your bird, the faster you can provide him with the right first aid. You will also need to keep a few things handy to help your bird in time. Here is a list of items that you must have in your bird's first aid kit:

- An emergency contact number
- Number and directions to your vet's clinic
- A pair of tweezers
- Gauze roll to wrap the bird
- Antibiotic cream
- Hydrogen peroxide
- Thermometer
- A heating pad or lamp
- A large towel to hold the bird
- Syringe or a medicine dropper
- Gloves to keep your hands safe if the bird is not hand tamed yet.
- Scissors
- Q-tip for ointment application
- Sterilized gauze to manage bleeding

- Styptic pencil or flour.

With these items in place you will not need to scramble and waste time when your bird does have an emergency. If you are leaving your bird under someone else's care, make sure you give them all the instructions required to take care of your bird in an emergency.

5. Can birds be insured?

Getting pet insurance for birds is not very easy. Most insurance companies will provide policies for cats and dogs, but rarely for birds. However, there are some reliable ones that will give you decent benefits. The most common things that are covered by popular pet insurance are:

- Veterinary charges: They will pay for certain diagnostic procedures like X-rays and even some consultation fees. Veterinarian costs will most include emergencies only. In the case of birds like the cockatiel that have long lives, there may be a limit on the cover offered annually that may go up to $1500 or £3000.

- Escape or Loss/ Death: If you lose your bird to theft or death, they may cover some amount of the market value of an exotic bird. Theft and Escape cover requires you to fulfill some security conditions such as purchasing a five-lever lock for the cage door.

- Public Liability: This covers any damage cause by your bird to another person or property.

- Overseas covers: This is necessary for you to travel with your pet to some countries.

The cost of your insurance with all these covers will come up to about $150 or £280 a month. These covers are purchased separately and you can cut costs on things like overseas cover or public liability cover if you do not think that it is necessary. However, all these covers are highly recommended for all pet owners. You can compare the costs of various insurance plans online to find one that works for you. If you have multiple birds, some of them may also offer a 10% discount on the insurance cover.

The two most popular insurance plans for parrots are:

Pet Assure: With this policy you can only have your bird checked by a vet in the network approved by them. If your vet is not part of this network, you need to find one that is or you will not be able to get the cover for vet costs.

VPI: This insurance does allow you to see any preferred veterinarian. However, they do put a limit on the number of visits and the cover that they offer annually. So, you may not be able to get full coverage for any major procedure that your bird may have to undergo.

That said, there is no policy for birds that is perfect, so if you want to choose the most reliable one it may be the one that your veterinarian is associated with. That way you can be assured of some cover at least.

Chapter 8: Cost of Owning a Cockatiel

Before committing to a cockatiel, make sure you have the financial stability to maintain one. With every impulse buy, it is only the bird that suffers. Here is a detailed breakdown of the possible costs associated with cockatiels.

- Cost of the Cockatiel: $80-300 or £45-200 depending on the age and the variety of the cockatiel.

- Cage: $350-600 or £150-400 depending on the features available and the size. This is a one-time investment and it is recommended that you get the best.

- Food: $40 or £25 a month.

- Toys: This really depends on the type of toys that you buy, but you will shell out a minimum of $30-50 or £15-25 for sturdy toys for your cockatiel.

- Wing clipping: If you get their wings clipped by someone else, then you will spend about $15 to £10 every four months.

- Veterinarian Costs: You will spend at least $50 or £30 per visit to your veterinarian. You can expect annual costs of about $1200 or £650 per year.

- Pet Insurance: Depending on the kinds of covers that you are getting, your pet insurance may cost anything between $150- 280 or £80- 150 a month.

Conclusion

I hope that this book has helped you make the right choices for you and your bird. The focus of this book is to ensure that you have a bird that is healthy and happy. For all the first time owners, I hope this book has simplified the process of understanding what your bird really needs.

Thank you for choosing this book. But above all, thank you for learning about your bird before making that commitment. That is the first step towards becoming a wonderful cockatiel parent.

Here is wishing you and your bird a great journey together. Make sure that you constantly upgrade the information that you have about your bird. That way, you can be sure that you are giving your feathered friend the best possible life.

References

As mentioned before, the more you learn about your bird, the better it is. You will find that the process of taking care of your bird becomes extremely simple when you are equipped with knowledge. One of the best resources available is the Internet. Here are some websites that are guaranteed to give you great insights in to the world of cockatiels.

- www.cockatielcottage.net
- www.problemparrots.co.uk
- www.vcahospitals.com
- www.cockatiel.com
- www.thatpetplace.com/cockatiels-article
- www.buildanaviary.com
- www.aboutcockatiels.com
- www.astepupbird.com
- www.thedailycockatiel.blogspot.com
- www.cockatiels4u.wordpress.com
- www.crazyforcockatiels.blogspot.com
- www.cockatielcove.tumblr.com
- www.pet.co.nz
- www.windycityparrot.com/blog
- www.innersouthvets.com.au
- www.pbspettravel.co.uk
- www.petlandkennesaw.com
- www.talkcockatiels.com
- www.tailfeathersnetwork.com
- www.ratforum.com
- www.totallytiels.com
- www.birdforum.net
- www.cockatielforum.com
- www.petsuppliesplusfl.com
- www.petcha.com
- www.parrotforums.com
- www.goodbirdinc.com
- www.associationofanimalbehaviorprofessionals.com
- www.beautyofbirds.com

- www.birdsnways.com
- www.board.birdchannel.com
- www.eol.org
- www.gopetsamerica.com
- www.webvet.com

Copyright and Trademarks: This publication is Copyrighted 2018 by Zoodoo Publishing. All products, publications, software and services mentioned and recommended in this publication are protected by trademarks. In such instance, all trademarks & copyright belong to the respective owners. All rights reserved. No part of this book may be reproduced or transferred in any form or by any means, graphic, electronic, or mechanical, including photocopying, recording, taping, or by any information storage retrieval system, without the written permission of the authors. Pictures used in this book are either royalty free pictures bought from stock-photo websites or have the source mentioned underneath the picture.

Disclaimer and Legal Notice: This product is not legal or medical advice and should not be interpreted in that manner. You need to do your own due-diligence to determine if the content of this product is right for you. The author and the affiliates of this product are not liable for any damages or losses associated with the content in this product. While every attempt has been made to verify the information shared in this publication, neither the author nor the affiliates assume any responsibility for errors, omissions or contrary interpretation of the subject matter herein. Any perceived slights to any specific person(s) or organization(s) are purely unintentional. We have no control over the nature, content and availability of the web sites listed in this book. The inclusion of any web site links does not necessarily imply a recommendation or endorse the views expressed within them. Zoodoo Publishing takes no responsibility for, and will not be liable for, the websites being temporarily unavailable or being removed from the Internet. The accuracy and completeness of information provided herein and opinions stated herein are not guaranteed or warranted to produce any particular results, and the advice and strategies, contained herein may not be suitable for every individual. The author shall not be liable for any loss incurred as a consequence of the use and application, directly or indirectly, of any information presented in this work. This publication is designed to provide information in regards to the subject matter covered. The information included in this book has been compiled to give an overview of the subject s and detail some of the symptoms, treatments etc. that are available to people with this condition. It is not intended to give medical advice. For a firm diagnosis of your condition, and for a treatment plan suitable for you, you should consult your doctor or consultant. The writer of this book and the publisher are not responsible for any damages or negative consequences following any of the treatments or methods highlighted in this book. Website links are for informational purposes and should not be seen as a personal endorsement; the same applies to the products detailed in this book. The reader should also be aware that although the web links included were correct at the time of writing, they may become out of date in the future.

www.ingramcontent.com/pod-product-compliance
Lightning Source LLC
Chambersburg PA
CBHW061450040426
42450CB00007B/1294